Designing with Grasses

Designing with Grasses

NEIL LUCAS

TIMBER PRESS
Portland · London

For my Mum,
who couldn't stay to see this book published.

Frontispiece: When used with more solid structural planting such as trees
and shrubs, grasses' lightness of form and almost-constant movement
perfectly complements the heaviness of the woody plants as seen here on
a misty October morning at Knoll Gardens in Dorset, England.

All photographs by Neil Lucas unless otherwise indicated.

Published in 2011 by Timber Press, Inc.

The Haseltine Building   2 The Quadrant
133 S.W. Second Avenue, Suite 450   135 Salusbury Road
Portland, Oregon 97204-3527   London NW6 6RJ
www.timberpress.com   www.timberpress.co.uk

Printed in China.
Text designed by Susan Applegate

Library of Congress Cataloguing-in-Publication Data

    Lucas, Neil, 1957–
    Designing with grasses Neil Lucas.—1st ed.
        p. cm.
    Includes bibliographical references and index.
    ISBN-13: 978-0-88192-983-6
    1. Ornamental grasses. 2. Gardens—Design. I. Title.
    SB431.7.L83 2011
    716—dc22   2010028453

A catalogue record for this book is also available from the British Library.

Contents

Foreword

THE PAST FEW DECADES have witnessed profound changes in the way we view our gardens, and in the ways we plant them, use them and maintain them. Our perennial affection for beauty is now matched with a growing desire for functionality. Gardens must be pretty and be purposeful. They should please our eyes, entertain us, take us places. They should also offer refuge and inspiration, and smartly practical spaces where we can simply live well. Above all, our gardens must do this with increased efficiency, using resources fairly and wisely and, whenever possible, giving something back by supporting the living communities that surround them. We want our gardens to work and we want them to require less work.

The astounding growth in the popularity of grasses during this same period is no coincidence. More than any other group in our vast garden palette, grasses can do more with less. The innate adaptability that has allowed grasses and their relatives, the sedges and rushes, to inhabit infinite niches around the globe makes them uniquely suited to the varied demands of modern gardens. Neil Lucas knows all of this firsthand, and he knows it well. In *Designing with Grasses* he has illustrated the ethos of a grassy style of gardening that is elegantly in sync with our time.

I originally met Neil through California plantsman Dave Fross, and was immediately impressed by his knowledge and delighted by his wit and generosity of spirit. We've since made many trips together through grass-filled landscapes and gardens in his native England and in North America, and I never fail to learn something in Neil's company. His refined eye is evident in his photographs: Neil can capture the grace and subtle midwinter drama of native moor grasses mingling with heathers in a Dorset meadow, or the joyful lilt of miscanthus plumes in his own Knoll Gardens in autumn.

Located near Wimborne in an enviably frosty bit of southern England, Knoll Gardens' four acres have served as Neil's proving grounds for myriad design and maintenance strategies and as the 'launch site' of nine consecutive Chelsea Gold Medal-winning exhibits of grasses. Knoll is also home to Neil's specialist nursery, which offers perhaps the most extensive selection of grasses in the U.K. The diversity of grasses that Neil has brought to Knoll has in turn enriched collections and displays in many private and public gardens including the Royal Horticultural Society Garden, Wisley.

Neil Lucas has a deep understanding of the breadth of possibilities for using grasses in landscapes, and has condensed all of his experience into a personal yet universally practical volume. His book is populated by rain gardens, roof gardens, gravel gardens, wetlands, meadows, urban centers and intimate home habitats. Throughout, the focus is on a proven palette of especially hardy plants, most of which are as well suited to North America as they are to the British Isles and northern Europe. For experienced gardeners as well as those who are just discovering grasses, *Designing with Grasses* offers a thoroughly modern perspective on the role of grasses in beautifully functional landscapes.

RICK DARKE
August 2010

Acknowledgements

I HAVE ALWAYS BEEN LUCKY, meeting people throughout my life who have been generous and willing to share their time, knowledge and friendship. If I were to thank all of these people adequately then this would be by far the most extensive part of the book.

However, special thanks must go to the team at Knoll Gardens, without whom neither the nursery nor the garden, nor indeed this book, would exist. To Ross Humphrey who runs the nursery and is my right-hand man for most things, and to Gary Fatt, Pat Humphrey, Pam Lel, Angela Mann, Luke Tanswell, Amanda Walker and Trevor Walker.

I wish to thank my mum and my stepdad, Janet and John Flude, who helped me to purchase Knoll in 1994, giving me the chance to fulfil my lifetime ambition of owning my own garden.

I am also grateful to Dave and Rainie Fross, whose enthusiasm, knowledge and long-term friendship continues to be a most special pleasure. And to Rick Darke and Melinda Zoehrer, for their generous help, friendship and advice on so many matters, I shall always remain truly grateful.

In the UK, I wish to thank David Jewell (whose passion for grasses equals my own), as well as Michelle Cleave and Tom Cope, Beth Chatto and David Ward, Jaimie Blake, John Coke, Chris Evans, Chris Greene, Jim Gardiner, Fergus Garrett, Ian Harris, Roy Lancaster, Caroline Legard, Ian LeGros, Anna Mumford, Keith Powrie, Becky Rochester and Cleve West. I wish to thank Erica Gordon-Mallin for her skilled editing, and Anne Crotty for her patient proofreading. Thanks are also due to Poul Petersen in Denmark.

In the United States, I am grateful to Ed and Lucie Snodgrass and to Jim Ault, Fred Ballerini, Sue Barton, Kurt Bluemel, Steve Castorani, Pat Cullina, Mike Curto, Melissa Fisher, Dale Hendricks, Casey Lyon, Bernard Trainor and Paul van Meter.

IMAGE ACKNOWLEDGEMENTS My special thanks to friend and photographer Dianna Jazwinski whose wonderful imagery graces many a page in this book. A warm thanks also to Rick Darke whose patience and willingness to share his great photographic knowledge helped enormously with my own rather limited abilities. My thanks also to Alexandre Bailhache, Rick Darke, Dave Fross, Ross Humphrey, Jason Liske, Ed Snodgrass and Amanda Walker for generously supplying images for use in the book.

I am also deeply indebted to many gardens both public and private, and to nurseries, reserves and institutions, for their help and advice with many of the images. Sincere thanks to The Beth Chatto Gardens, Chanticleer Garden, Chicago Botanic Garden, Longwood Gardens, Lurie Garden, North Creek Nurseries, Royal Botanic Gardens at Kew, Royal Horticultural Society Gardens at Wisley and Hyde Hall, Scampston Hall and the Springs Preserve.

THE KNOLL GARDENS FOUNDATION My own journey is now inextricably bound up with my garden. To this end, and hopefully to the advantage of us both, I have been lucky enough to establish a charitable organization called the The Knoll Gardens Foundation, dedicated not just to the preservation of the gardens but to the continuation of everything that goes into making a successful garden—to the ethos that drives it forward and to that essential spirit of relentlessly optimistic experimentation and learning, without which we achieve nothing.

ONE
Discovering Grasses

When I was a child, my grandfather was very keen on delphiniums and during my summer visits to his expansive garden I came to love them too. Uninspiring mounds of green foliage would gradually form tall, graceful, towering spikes of colour that, at least in the earlier years, towered over the top of my head. Some of my earliest memories involve being captivated by the sheer beauty of the flowers, the colours and the way they were arranged on the stems. In time I started my own plant collections, expanding to dahlias and delphiniums, and would spend hours observing their mind-boggling variety of shape, form and colour. I became transfixed by my plants' growing cycles—the complex processes they underwent in the course of a single season, and the way they would react differently to the various conditions that could exist in the same garden.(Grass, on the other hand, was merely for walking on.)

Growing up and beginning to explore in earnest, I visited as many gardens as I could, increasingly enchanted by these magical places where lots of different plants grew together. While most of my friends aspired to become train drivers and secret agents, I dreamt of becoming a gardener and eventually having my own garden. I spent every possible moment around plants and people who knew about them.

Tough, adaptable grasses will happily tolerate less-than-hospitable urban situations. By this riverside in New York, *Panicum virgatum* brings a natural touch to what might otherwise be an unpromising hardscape—for humans as well as other forms of life. Photograph courtesy of Ross Humphrey.

Developing My Approach

By the time I came to Knoll Gardens in Dorset, my love affair with plants as individuals had been supplanted by a fascination with gardens as systems or communities of plants, and the processes that make them work. Having spent years looking after gardens professionally for others, I had witnessed the most attractive of plants become ugly and disappointing under conditions that they did not like. I came to understand that seeing the garden as a whole, with its various moods and conditions, was just as important as understanding the plants that go in it.

'Right plant, right place' is a simple practical maxim encouraging us to choose plants that will best suit the conditions available. So many gardens fail because this simple piece of common sense is ignored or forgotten. Certainly soil can be improved, water added and climatic factors softened to some extent, but essentially for a garden to be successful its plants must be happy with, or at least able to tolerate, the prevailing cultural conditions.

Knoll, for instance, was originally a private botanical collection, principally containing woody plants drawn from around the world; while many like the eucalyptus and euonymus took to the garden's generally dry, sandy conditions, others such as the collection of rhododendrons needed copious amounts of water and feeding to survive and prosper. Once this level of care was stopped, it became obvious that these rhododendrons would not thrive in the garden's conditions if left on their own, so they have since been largely removed.

WHY GRASSES?　At first woody plants were my gardening mainstay, but I later found that grasses were effective in the garden for nearly as long as the woody plants were—and that grasses provided not only structure and form but also movement and a range of talents to perfectly complement most other plants. Grasses were also versatile and adaptable, capable of growing on sandy soils or heavy clay, in sun or shade, in pools or other wet areas and even among root systems under trees. And when used together in larger informal drifts they created a feeling of relaxed naturalness that, to me, hinted strongly at childhood days spent on coasts and other exciting, invigorating and untamed grassy places.

As if this were not enough, I soon found that a 'naturalistic' approach to gardening spearheaded by the use of grasses led to noticeably *less work* than I had been accustomed to doing. (The term 'naturalistic' can be used to describe a generally less formal approach to the layout and design of plantings, where a limited but well-chosen palette of plants is used for maximum effect with minimal work.) Not having to constantly deadhead, stake, tidy and spray slowly encouraged a subtly different sort of environment—one perhaps just beginning to mimic the flavour of an established natural system, which a greater variety of wildlife seemed to find attractive. As I drew upon an ever-widening palette of grasses, their usefulness and adaptability became clear.

GRASSES AND THE BIGGER PICTURE   Grasses are a worldwide success story—a huge group of plants with more than ten thousand different species in their own family, and with the grass allies such as sedges and rushes contributing at least half that number again. They are arguably the most successful group of plants on the planet, covering more ground and feeding more wildlife than any other group. In our natural systems, grasses and their allies can be found on virtually every landmass, in every region, in every locality and on every soil type. Wherever there is plant life, grasses are almost certain to have a local representative.

Like many gardeners, designers and conservationists working today, I have come to realize that gardens can be more than just decoration. To be sure they are pleasant havens to be relaxed in and admired, but as our understanding of the world evolves, perhaps so do our attitudes towards gardening.

We are learning about biodiversity, the all-embracing term for all forms of life including mammals, birds, insects and plants. And we are learning about our collective effect on all of these living things; as sensitive and environmentally savvy gardeners, we are trying not to waste valuable long-term resources on short-term horticultural effects.

While much of the countryside is regarded as green open space, farmland and gardens with large expanses of tightly cut turfgrass, including golf courses, can become effective monocultures that are austere places for most other forms of life.

We are learning that continually taking over natural areas for our own use puts increased pressure on the remaining natural systems—and that the intricacy and interrelatedness of these systems can be all too easily interrupted, yet not so easily mended.

Above all, we are learning that our gardens and designed spaces increasingly constitute a significant part of the Earth's remaining green space, and that our gardens are therefore gaining a value that could never have been imagined by previous generations of gardeners. As we rely on our natural systems to support us for food, shelter and the air we breathe, we are inextricably bound up with the plants, insects and animals that make up our world's biodiversity. As natural habitats are destroyed and the natural landscape is built up, the value of our gardens increases—if we design these outdoor spaces conscientiously. Although they cannot be a replacement for natural ecosystems, our gardens can serve as a partial substitute, providing a place for the plants, insects and animals on which we ourselves depend.

Understanding grasses' origins and their contributions to the wider ecosystem inspires us see our gardens differently. Grasses can offer us insight into a way of working—an approach to gardening that combines a focus on adaptability, ease of use and sheer simplicity with the most strikingly beautiful of effects.

BLURRING AND MERGING   If asked to sum up what I have learned through gardening with grasses so far, I think I would have to invent a new phrase: 'blur and merge'.

It is in our interests to blur the lines between our natural systems and our designed spaces, and grasses are perhaps the perfect group of plants to help us do this. Natural systems offer well-adjusted, self-renewing, evolving communities while our gardens are all too often the very opposite; we have much to learn from them. The principles we see operating so successfully in nature can be mirrored in our designed spaces with real benefits.

And we can merge our love of short-term interest with longer-term satisfaction. Blowsy summertime flowers are wonderful, but not at the price of boring nothingness for the rest of the year. Gardens can and should be of interest at all times.

Grasses are found in virtually
every area from high mountain-
top to seashore, and they play an
important role in today's modern,
low-maintenance, nature-tolerant
gardens. This naturally occurring meadow in Utah's Zion
National Park (above) is a balanced, self-renewing plant community from which we can draw
inspiration for our gardens.

Rather than lawn grass and surrounding borders or flowerbeds,
this garden area (right) has
merged these traditional features,
resulting in a meadow effect.
Not only is the area fun to play
in and explore but it is also easier
to maintain and gives a greater
sense of space and openness.

We can blur the often-sacrosanct lines between border and lawn, between trimmed hedge and natural shelter. Narrow borders and tightly cut lawns are static and unchanging, and moreover they are usually hard work. Blending borders, lawns and pathways creates a feeling of space and dynamism. And it allows plants to do more of the work.

We can merge our focus on plants as individuals with the cultivation of the garden as a whole. Far greater success, and for less effort, can be achieved by cultivating the garden as a community, rather than seeing plants as a series of unrelated individuals.

We can blur our search for horticultural perfection with the acceptance of practicality. Plants that need constant attention by way of spraying, staking, deadheading, watering and general cosseting in

The designer of this Carmel garden, on the Pacific Coast of California, has successfully blurred the line between lawn and border to create a pleasing combination of sedges and a grass, *Koeleria macrantha*, that has been used as a low-maintenance substitute for more traditional turf grass.

In this golf links (above), low-maintenance native sedges and grasses grow close to the traditionally maintained links without compromising the integrity of the playing surface.

A crisp, well-maintained lawn (right) can be a thing of beauty, but many are now questioning the validity of this long-established tradition, especially where such features are expensive in terms of the time and precious resources needed to maintain them.

order to give anything in return are for the most part just hard work—and often unnecessary, when so many plants will exist happily with almost no attention.

We can also merge our conception of indoor rooms with outdoor spaces. While we lavish much care and attention on our indoor rooms, our outdoor spaces benefit from similar care. Basic garden design is not a fashion accessory—it is merely a thought process intended to make the best use of finite space and resources, and it is a valuable tool for any gardener.

How to Use this Book

Simply using grasses in the garden is no panacea in itself. But grasses' inclination towards success under so many different and sometimes challenging conditions, and the feelings and effects they evoke though a happy combination of individual beauty and mass effect, make them incredibly valuable.

This book is about the grasses that I enjoy, and how to use them in our gardens and designed spaces. It is also about why we might *want* to use grasses, and it looks to our natural systems for that answer.

This book is not just for established gardeners; it is for anyone who takes an interest in outdoor spaces, whether surrounding a small private home or in a larger public space. With an eye towards naturalistic gardening and environmental awareness, I hope to explore how such a worldwide success story as the family of grasses can be used so effectively and easily in our gardens.

Grasses and their potential in planting design is a huge subject which no single book can claim to comprehensively cover. But it is my hope that the following pages will provide you with a real flavour—a taste of the amazing opportunities that this versatile and beautiful group of plants has to offer.

TWO
A Natural Community of Grasses

WHILE 'COMMUNITY', 'SEASONALITY' and 'rhythm' may not be the very first terms that come to mind when we think of gardening, they evoke important concepts that can shape our gardens into more satisfying places. Understanding a garden's cultural conditions—acid or alkaline, wet or dry soils; sun or shade, warm or cold, windy or sheltered—and choosing plants best suited to these conditions is essential for creating long-term and successful plantings. But a garden is also subject to other influences which may not be so obvious or clear-cut. Some of the most inspirational gardens—those that have the 'wow' factor, imparting a special sense of place or even magic—are the ones that are cultivated as whole communities of plants rather than as a collection of sometimes-disconnected individual specimens. These gardens encourage natural rhythms within their plantings; they are in tune with their surroundings, and in this sense they work with nature rather than battling against it. With their amazing versatility and adaptability, grasses

On a clear December morning following a cold night, the frost on the dried flower stems of tufted hair grass, *Deschampsia cespitosa* (background), creates a magical, transient and almost ethereal effect in this riverside meadow in Exeter, Devon. The hard rush, *Juncus inflexus* (foreground), also thrives in even wetter parts of the meadow and provides solidity of form in successful contrast to the airiness of the hair grass.

can be important tools for achieving this kind of balanced, satisfying garden—where the gardener's role is more akin to that of an editor than an enforcer.

Seasonality and Rhythm

'Seasonality' refers to the processes that plants and therefore gardens undergo in response to the changing conditions of the local climate over the course of a year. It is also responsible for the essence of a garden's 'rhythm'—a series of naturally induced changes that happen over the course of a year as the garden and its plants react to seasonal changes in light, temperature and weather patterns. Through recognizing and celebrating the seasonal variations in a garden, we open up a whole new series of possibilities for our designed landscapes. In a garden, seasonal change is inevitable, strongly desirable and arguably the single most important component of the garden's natural rhythm.

For instance, the Mill End borders at Knoll were designed specifically with a narrow snaking bark path so that visitors could enjoy the plants at relatively close quarters, watching and admiring the sometimes rapid, sometimes subtle changes as the seasons progressed. In spring, after the area has been cut to the ground, quickly recovering clumps of arundo, miscanthus, pennisetum, calamagrostis and panicum along with other perennials, such as eupatorium, geranium and persicaria, rapidly clothe the bare earth. As poppies and foxgloves flower, so does what must be the earliest of fountain grasses—the admirable *Pennisetum massaicum* 'Red Buttons'. Well known for its early-flowering nature, the initially bright red flowers held on long slender stalks are quite distinctive and will continue to flower, at least in good soils, right through into autumn. As high summer approaches the *Arundo donax* specimens reach their full majestic height in concert with their associated perennials while miscanthus, panicum and pennisetum are in full, fabulous, flower before gradually descending into their more subtle garb of beige with the onset of autumn's first frosts. With the coming of winter the skeletal remains of the plants take on yet another form with a covering of snow or even heavy frosts. Almost every day of the year this border has something interesting to offer.

Grasses, especially the wide-ranging deciduous group, are excellent seasonal indicators as they perform their annual miracle of fast green growth, magnificent flower and autumnal tints followed by their winter brown coats standing tall and resolute until the following spring. Then the whole process is repeated, revealing a time-honoured dynamic equilibrium where in the midst of constant change the annual rhythm remains constant.

In gardens that are severely formal in layout, where hardscape and design considerations outweigh the plant content, there is far less opportunity to celebrate seasonal change. Where there is intentionally a much tighter control of seasonal change and therefore of nature itself, through the use of features like formal parterres and terraces with their hard surfaces, tightly clipped evergreen hedges and perhaps bedding schemes limited to two changes a year, it is more difficult to introduce seasonality without a major revision of the original design concept. On a larger, public scale, such comparatively austere layouts may have a place as historical museum pieces, but in my view they are increasingly less relevant to the needs of the modern-day gardener.

Similarly, gardens that consist largely of an expanse of purposeless resource-hungry lawn grass, framed perhaps by narrow and mostly empty borders, have been responsible for the coining of the term 'green desert'. Not a term of endearment, it takes issue with the repetitive and unchanging nature of the design. Even when decorated with the occasional evergreen to provide 'year-round interest' the effect is often the reverse of our intentions.

A garden that honours seasonality and conveys a sense of rhythm is easy to achieve, especially with informal designs, if we follow a few simple guidelines:

• Think big. A few well-chosen features covering a larger area are more effective and easier to look after long-term than many separate smaller features, which can look fussy and ill-considered. For

Having been cut back in late March, the borders at Knoll are already a creative tapestry of colours and leaf shapes by May (top left). By early summer (bottom left), foxgloves, poppies and geraniums join the first of the grasses such as *Pennisetum thunbergii* 'Red Buttons' and *Molinia caerulea* subsp. *caerulea* 'Edith Dudszus' in flower. In August (above), pathways are defined by the plants which have reached their mature height. Perennials such as eupatoriums, echinaceas and persicarias join panicums, pennisetum and miscanthus in a high summer extravaganza of flower and form. The following February (left), several inches of snow freshen the pathways, highlighting the brown skeletal outlines of the giant reed, *Arundo donax*, alongside eupatoriums, panicums, sedums and pennisetum.

instance, choose a meadow that merges into a taller border that also acts as a screen over a hodgepodge of separate lawns, borders and plantings. Thinking big is especially important in more diminutive gardens, where small lawns, small borders and small plants add up to a small effect.

- If possible, hardscape such as paving and concrete should comprise a smaller portion of your garden than plants and soft surfaces.
- Remove or downsize the tightly cut lawn, or at least relax your maintenance regime and allow it to grow longer.
- Lose any tightly clipped shrubs and hedges that serve no purpose.
- Choose plants for a purpose, such as hakonechloa to cover tree bases in shade, carex to form the base of a meadow, or pennisetums to provide summer flower in dry sun—and let them do most of the work.

EDITING IN THE GARDEN   So often in our attempts to create the perfect garden, or even the perfect low-maintenance garden, we exercise too much control and ignore the natural processes that can help us achieve our goals more satisfactorily and with less effort and heartache.

It has been said before that gardeners achieve best results when acting more as 'editors' than as 'enforcers'. If we find we are constantly battling with nature through constantly trying to supervise every action in the garden, then we are simply attempting to exert too much control. Working with rather than against nature; understanding and taking advantage of natural processes; and regarding the garden as a whole rather than a number of disparate areas and features is more likely to produce the most satisfying garden, for the gardener who cares for it as well as those who visit it.

THE YEAR-ROUND GARDEN   For many gardeners in temperate climates, spring and summer is *the* period to enjoy the garden. This is when popular flowers such as roses as well as annual bedding plants like marigolds, begonias and petunias are at their peak. But in focusing on such beautiful, showy, colourful and yet transient plants we sometimes neglect to include plants that are of interest and have a value at other times of the year. After the blowsy summertime period ends, our gardens can seem to languish, virtually forgotten and even unloved, until the following season.

Adding grasses to the garden's mix of plants keeps the interest flowing over a much longer period. Take, for example, the prairie switch grass *Panicum virgatum*; the species, or any of its gardenworthy cultivars, provides green mounds in the early part of the year which act as a foil and a background for spring-flowering plants. By midsummer, though still playing a background role, its tall upright foliage begins to show buds. These later blossom into myriad tiny flowers that are again set off by the foliage, which can turn some amazing warm fall colours. Then, finally, the whole plant—stems, leaves and flowers—dries to a strawy beige and this colour is retained through most of the winter along with the plant's outline, lending a warm hue as well as structure to the garden for at least nine months out of the year.

Grasses contribute such long-term effects to the gardens in mediterranean climates too, although as the seasons are markedly different winter dormancy is effectively replaced by summer dormancy. For example, the delicate-looking mosquito grass, *Bouteloua gracilis*, would go strawy and dormant in cooler temperate areas during the winter period whereas if left to its own devices in warmer climates it would become strawy and close down during the hottest summer period.

Some of the major grasses used in gardens, including *Miscanthus*, *Panicum* and *Pennisetum*, are all deciduous and contribute fresh flower, mature size and shape around high summer to early autumn—just when so many other garden plants are quieting down. Combined with later-flowering perennials and then autumn-colouring woody plants, this period could be considered the absolute peak of performance for this group of grasses. However, rather like a good malt whisky, the aftertaste can be long and warming; from a high peak of perfection there is a long and dignified descent through subtle and spectacular autumnal colourings to the final garb of winter brown and beige tones of the dried skeletal stems and flowers. All the while these grasses contribute shape, movement and subtle colourations to garden scenes so often otherwise bereft of such pleasures.

Through the use of grasses, gardens can be as pleasurable in the autumn and winter months as they are during the hectic and heady

days of spring and early summer. Grasses' resilience, movement and quiet beauty bring a serene and graceful quality to our gardens' autumn and winter performance that is virtually unique to these versatile plants. Then, on occasion, when backed by low winter sunshine or when outlined with heavy frost, this background role converts to a commanding presence with a display of delicate beauty rivalling the spring or summer displays that any other group of garden plants can muster. Grasses allow us to enjoy our gardens when most more traditional garden plants are least interesting.

Grasses and Companion Plants

Grasses are very sociable plants. Rather like heathers or geraniums, they happily accept close planting in groups and are often most striking and effective in the garden or wider landscape when viewed en masse. In close up a grass may be beautiful, but when grown in a bold group it can look simply breathtaking. Used well, grasses' sociability can help us to see the garden as a living entity—showing that it is the community as a whole that matters more than the individual plants.

In our natural landscapes we recognize and admire communities of plants that have adapted to the conditions of a specific environment, whether on a cliff face, in a prairie or in a redwood forest. In our designed spaces, the hand of nature is necessarily replaced by the hand of the gardener. But the gardener's hand can be guided by the principles we see operating so successfully in nature.

Much like people, plants mostly prefer living in communities; they need a suitable place and a worthwhile function in order to give their best. Where plants are grown solely for their individual qualities rather than with an eye toward the part they play in a larger scheme, this could be more accurately termed a collection rather than a garden or a community.

For many, a garden really is something more than just a physical space; it is a combination of different elements brought together, not always intentionally, to create something truly greater than the sum of its parts. At least to some degree, such gardens are created to celebrate the joy, the delight and the fascination we find not just in the individual

Deciduous grasses in particular can exhibit marked differences in their appearance as the seasons alter. Introduced by John Greenlee of California, the fountain grass hybrid *Pennisetum* 'Fairy Tails', seen here, has generously produced, exquisitely delicate pinkish flowers when seen close-up and in fresh flower (top left). As the season progresses, the flower colour fades but is replaced by an attractive mature form with a desirable, gently pendulous habit (top right). Later still, as autumn moves imperceptibly into winter, the whole plant dries to its winter outfit that can be lit up to spectacular effect by low winter sunshine (bottom). Top left photograph courtesy of Dianna Jazwinski.

Many grasses are able to remain standing through winter. In December at Knoll Gardens, low winter sunshine brings out the delicate yet resilient beauty of *Miscanthus* and *Panicum* specimens, which can rival the spring or summer displays of other garden plants.

plants but in the natural systems, the checks and balances, the annual rhythms that make up both our designed spaces and the natural world with which so many of us feel a deep connection. In this sense, a garden is an outdoor place where aesthetics and practicality, diversity and restraint, converge in a harmonious whole: a functioning community.

The Spaces Between: Natural Ground Cover

Almost as important as the plants we use in our gardens are the spaces that we leave between them, and yet so often this essential element is neglected or overlooked. In nature, bare patches of ground seldom stay

A variety of materials can be used effectively as
surface mulch, which not only keeps weeds down and
retains water, but also allows for a decorative surface
between plants to form part of the garden scene.
Clockwise from top left are: gravel and pebble, leaf
litter and bark, pine needles, and sand and gravel.

Using a similar material as a practical and decorative finish for both planted and non-planted areas softens the traditionally clear division between paths, lawns and borders. This in itself can lend the area a more inviting and relaxed feel. Where a naturally occurring material such as fallen pine needles can be utilized close to its point of origin, an even greater sense of place can be achieved.

bare for long, yet many gardeners assiduously clear the surface of a border or other planting area, leaving expanses of bare ground. Removing all debris, leaf litter and organic matter requires considerable maintenance and fails to conserve rainwater or other important and freely available resources. As Doug Tallamy writes in *Bringing Nature Home*: "We lose much when we remove leaf litter because it provides so many free services for us; free mulch, free fertilizer, free weed control and free soil amendments".

The space in between plants is such an important part of our garden landscape, and a sympathetic surface covering acts as a practical foil, a frame and a setting for the chosen plants. The right ground cover should be not only visually attractive but also easy to maintain and effective in bringing cohesion to a border or planting. The right ground cover gives plantings a sense of place, and plants an air of belonging.

Any kind of organic material such as chipped bark, stable manure, straw, bracken, garden compost or simple fallen leaves can be used and all contribute to the fertility and general health of the soil. The layer need not be thick; a few centimetres (or one to two inches) would suffice, though it can be a bit thicker among larger plants. Inorganic materials such as gravel, slate or chippings do not really improve the soil directly but still conserve essential moisture and when used well are very effective aesthetically.

The manner in which a surface material is used also has a major influence on a garden. Clear divisions between lawns, paths and planted areas can be effective and satisfying in some situations but in others a looser approach is more fitting. At Knoll Gardens we allow 'soft' paths to meander through larger plantings, blurring the edges between walkways and planted areas by using bark or pine needles. It brings an air of relaxed naturalness, and is so easy to maintain. To achieve this effect it is often easiest to regard the area as a single planting and thread the pathway through simply by leaving more space between the plants where the pathway is desired.

THREE
Designing with Grasses

ALL GARDENS ARE made up of a combination of different elements, of building blocks that need to be put together in the right mix to make a successfully designed whole. By designing with an eye towards screening, structural planting, open spaces (whether grassy or hard surface), planted areas and borders, pathways and viewpoint, we can really make the most of our gardens. And when it comes to garden design, grasses are a real boon; unlike lawn grass, which at best offers a year-round flat, static, emerald green carpet, ornamental grasses are endlessly versatile building blocks that can be used in many situations and for a range of different purposes.

Grasses as Building Blocks

Backbone, foundation or structural planting generally refers to the practice of using plants to create a permanent framework in the garden—for instance, dividing up the space through internal boundaries or using plantings to separating one's garden from the neighbours'. Woody plants such as trees, shrubs and hedges are ideal for creating

The ability to remain standing well into the winter, absorbing and reflecting even the slightest amount of sunshine, makes grasses such as *Panicum virgatum* ideal companions to evergreens and other woody backbone shrubs. Here the grasses lighten and enliven an otherwise dull winter corner at Knoll Gardens.

structure, as they remain present and contribute to the landscape all year round.

The perfect companions to this essential group of structural plants, grasses offer a range of talents that will immeasurably improve a garden's year-round performance. For example, much foundation or backbone planting can consist of relatively solid, to the point of uninteresting and even boring, evergreens. Much as these evergreens perform an essential function of shelter and screening, using grasses along with evergreens is an easy and effective way of bringing some life and interest, some colour and change, to what can otherwise be static or dull layouts. Larger specimen trees, while hardly boring or uninteresting, can have bare empty spaces below that can be enriched and enlivened by some shade-loving grasses. Even well-designed areas of woody plants can benefit from the addition of grasses simply because their sinuous shape and form, their distinct line and almost-continuous movement, work so well with woody companions.

Ornamental grasses are the ultimate mood setters or stage managers. Gardens have been likened to a theatre set where scenes are changed as the production moves through different locations; of all the plants, I find that grasses signal a season change most dramatically as they move from new spring growth to lush summer flowering before their statuesque winter finale. Grasses are great at setting scenes and establishing an atmosphere or ambience in which other plants can also thrive.

Although they can have a relatively understated demeanour, grasses display a variety of talents that make them useful to the gardener and designer. Once identified and understood, their characteristics can make a huge difference to our gardens, and are so very easy to use successfully.

Grasses and Sunlight

Very few groups of plants are transformed as dramatically as grasses by the effects of different kinds of light. Shafts of afternoon sunlight striking even a single blade of grass can imbue the plant with a magical quality. Many light conditions react with grasses to create entrancing performances using sunlight and shadow, evoking mystery and intrigue

in the process. An expansive planting, when backlit by low sunshine in either morning or afternoon, quite literally glows and radiates with light reflected from translucent stems, flowers and leaves. The effect is intensified still further by even the slightest breeze.

Grasses that really make the most of the light are the ones whose flowers are held clear above the foliage, allowing them to take full advantage of the reflected sunlight. A real favourite in this respect is *Calamagrostis brachytricha* whose large arrow-like heads of flowers point skyward and almost glow in the low sunlight. But there are also many others from which to choose. The fountain grasses or pennisetums, with their masses of fluffy caterpillar-like flowers, also excel. The rounded habit of *Pennisetum alopecuroides* 'Hameln' can be very effective as can the comparatively upright spikes of *Pennisetum* 'Fairy Tails'.

Few plants have the ability to transform their appearance so magnificently as grasses when backlit, particularly by low sunlight, as seen here early in the morning in the grass garden of the Royal Botanic Gardens Kew, London, in October. The tall cylindrical flowerheads of *Pennisetum macrourum* seem to burst up and outwards like a firework display, while *Eragrostis*, *Bouteloua* and *Stipa* provide froth and effervescence below.

As so many grass flowers remain intact for very long periods (above), their ability to provide sudden spectacular sunlight-fuelled performances lasts well into the winter. These pennisetum and miscanthus in the growing field at Knoll Gardens are still in pristine condition, highlighted by early January sunshine after a hard frost the previous night.

In the beautiful and tranquil Pennsylvania garden of Rick Darke and Melinda Zoehrer (right), a single *Calamagrostis brachytricha* specimen growing happily in partial shade is spotlighted by a shaft of transient afternoon sunlight—a regular matinée performance, needing only sunshine to provide a season's worth of interest.

Panicum, *Eragrostis* and *Molinia* are all equally responsive to light and the combination of all these different flower shapes when seen together, such as in the growing field at Knoll Gardens on a sunny winter's morning, is a sight not soon forgotten.

Such sunlight-fuelled performances are easy to achieve simply by placing grasses so they will be viewed with sunlight behind them at some point in the day. These brief but regular performances can then be enjoyed throughout a significant part of the year.

Colour and Continuity

Colour is an essential element in a successful garden, but it should not be sought at the expense of other equally desirable elements such as shape and year-round interest. All grasses produce flowers but it is the deciduous grasses like *Miscanthus*, *Panicum* and *Pennisetum* that provide the 'wow' factor so often associated with our garden displays.

Flower colour can range from the purples common to the panicums through the many shades of red that are found in bothriochloa, miscanthus and the pennisetums. Then there are an almost infinite number of pink, cream and white shades present in most major groups of grasses. Yellows can be found among the fresh flowers of the sedges such as *Carex elata* 'Aurea', and even shades of blue are seen in the likes of *Festuca glauca* in any of its forms and in *Poa labillardierei*, which boasts both foliage and flowers in matching shades of blue.

Unlike the colour provided by flowering plants that generally lasts for a relatively short if spectacular period, the colour provided by grasses can last many seasons. Many go through subtle changes of colour to provide a succession of interest that makes them excellent indicators of seasonal change as well as long-term garden performers.

For example, *Miscanthus sinensis* 'Ferner Osten' starts its growing cycle with green mounds of foliage that increase in bulk and height almost daily for the first half of the year. During the longest days of the year flower buds appear, eventually opening to one of the darkest red flowers available, set off beautifully by the lush green foliage. As weeks pass, the red fades to burnished silver while the leaves turn a warm burnt orange to provide a second combination of colours that is no less

effective than the first. Finally, in late autumn, the different colours fade away to leave the flowers, stems and leaves in many shades of straw and beige—yet another tasteful ensemble that lasts right through the winter period.

The term 'successional planting' is used to describe a long-established technique of using a series of different plants, often annuals, to flower one after another to give a succession of interest. Although very successful when done well, successional planting can also be very labour intensive. You can achieve the same effect with much less effort by planting a grass like *Miscanthus sinensis* 'Ferner Osten', which will provide you with a season's worth of interest from just one permanent plant.

Texture and Shape

Despite being often overlooked, the textural qualities of most flowering grasses can contribute much to the garden scene. Bear in mind that the flowers of most grasses will remain intact for many months after the initial flush of colour has long since faded, so if they have a textural quality or fine shape they will provide interest and pleasure for longer. For example, *Miscanthus sinensis* 'Flamingo', a first-class garden plant, has the most elegant, delicately pendulous flowers that are coloured a superb deep pink when first open; although this fresh colour soon fades, the shapely qualities of the flower remain and are arguably almost more effective than the first flush of colour.

Grasses stand out among perennials for their distinct quality of shape and form—their linear distinctiveness. Whether in association with other broadleaved plants, against more solid inanimate objects or in larger grasses-only plantings, the characteristic linear outline helps to create cohesion of design while allowing for light and easy movement. *Miscanthus sinensis* 'Morning Light' is often used as a single specimen where its unique vase-shaped outline is always distinctive, especially when contrasted against a more solid background. But as grasses are very sociable plants that will happily accept close grouping with their fellows without losing impact, nearly all will be even more effective when planted in larger groups.

Deer grass (*Muhlenbergia rigens*), for example, is one of the most

In full flower in August at Knoll Gardens, *Miscanthus sinensis* 'Ferner Osten' is among the darkest of cultivars, contrasting with the purple-topped angular stems of *Verbena bonariensis* (top). Two months later in October (bottom), while the verbena remains virtually the same, the miscanthus has undergone changes to flower and foliage, providing a dynamic procession of colour, texture and contrast for many months.

elegant of grasses, especially for warmer climates or drier soils where it produces fountains of narrow stems that spill outward in a neverending cascade. Although superb as mature individual plants, their effect is magnified and even more stunning when used en masse. With such generous performers as the deer grass it is important not to plant individuals too close together within the groups for fear of cramping their style. Contrastingly, the purple moor grass, *Molinia caerulea*, which has a more upright habit, appears happy with virtually any spacing.

As a rule the flowers of evergreen grasses and grass-like plants are less than striking, but this is more than compensated by the sculptural qualities of the foliage that is generally present for the whole year. Some of the sedges, including *Carex divulsa*, *C. testacea*, *C. dipsacea*, *C. secta* and *C. tenuiculmis*, excel in this respect; their flowers are sometimes considered insignificant (though actually close up they are fascinating), but their foliage has a remarkable form that is invaluable in the garden.

Grasses' distinct lines form a satisfying longlasting contrast with more solid objects, whether organic or inorganic. Here *Hakonechloa macra* is used successfully in association with seating and other hard surfaces in Battery Park, New York City.

Closely planted, evergreen *Carex testacea* provides a very textural surface reminiscent of waves.

Meadows and Lawns

Traditional tightly cut lawns that effectively serve no purpose other than being occasionally walked on are expensive to maintain, in terms of both time and resources. Replacing the lawn grass, or even just a section of a larger area, with a mixture of ornamental grasses and sedges creates an open grassy place—a meadow, which can become a sensory delight, a home for wildlife and an exciting place for play or simply passing through. Even on a small scale, a simple meadow can turn a staid patch of lawn grass into something infinitely more dynamic and interesting.

At the heart of many such meadows are the evergreen sedges. *Carex praegracilis* and *C. divulsa* are popular but most evergreen sedges can be

Replacing water-hungry lawn grass with easygoing evergreens such as sedges creates a relaxed, natural-feeling low-maintenence meadow which plants, people and wildlife can all enjoy.

used, their easygoing nature providing a solid base from which many other plants including bulbs, perennials and other grasses can grow. *Carex flacca*, the carnation sedge, makes quite stunning blue-grey carpets and will even cope with light shade.

Among the deciduous grasses there is a wide choice and it is always good practice to mix some of these in with the evergreens, even if simply as accent plants. In cooler climates, the quaking grass, *Briza media*, with its tiny but perfectly formed spikelets fluttering in the slightest breeze, is a delight in early summer and then *Deschampsia cespitosa*, in any one of its forms, produces a haze of flower later in the season to sublime effect. For warmer climates *Aristida purpurea* and species of *Nassella* and *Bouteloua* provide the same hazy beauty. Some of the larger-leaved 'blues' such as *Leymus condensatus* 'Canyon Prince' or *Elymus magellanicus* contrast very effectively with the greens of the sedges.

Repetition

Repeated use of a single plant, or several similar ones, is an effective way of giving a garden a theme or recognizable pattern. Repeated plants sometimes become known as signature plants because they give a planting its particular identity. Being quick-growing and amenable to close grouping, and with their distinctive linear outline, grasses are well placed to excel in this role. Any of the larger grasses such as *Miscanthus*, *Panicum*, *Saccharum* or *Calamagrostis*, and even the some-times-overplanted and often-maligned pampas *Cortaderia selloana* are all excellent for this purpose. While on a smaller scale, perhaps at the front of borders, *Nassella tenuissima*, *Eragrostis curvula*, *Helictotrichon sempervirens* or *Pennisetum orientale*, or perhaps *Hakonechloa macra* for more shady areas, are easy and very effective.

Movement and Sound

Whether through graceful movement provoked by a delicate summer's breeze or when being battered by severe winter gales, the lithe, flexing, almost-continuous motion and rustling sounds of stems, leaves and flowers is a prime attribute of the grass family. Highly evocative of

Using repeated groups of the same type of plant can bring unity to a planting. A free-flowering miscanthus is used along a city street in New York (above) with striking effect. On a smaller scale, but no less effectively, repeated groups of *Nassella tenuissima* (right) help to bring together differing groups of perennials in a new planting at the RHS Garden Wisley.

fabulous natural landscapes, such as coastal reed beds on a windy day, the sound and movement of grasses in our designed spaces breathes life into landscapes that can otherwise appear static and stationary. One of the common names for *Briza media* is quaking grass, which is particularly apt as the flowers not only move in the slightest breeze but rustle seductively. This is especially noticeable once they have gone straw-like and dry.

Grasses are seldom if ever heavy; their almost constantly moving stems are produced in great profusion, which even at height and when topped with flower manage to convey an airy lightness almost unequalled in the plant world. *Panicum virgatum* and its many cultivars are expert at creating this light and airy effect as they produce quite literally masses of tiny flowers that appear to hang, cloud-like, above the stems and leaves and are the perfect foil for more solid and inanimate partners.

Grasses' tendency to move in the slightest breeze, lending both movement and sound to otherwise static landscapes, can be especially valuable in urban areas where their softness and pliability act as an antidote to the frequently overpowering solidity of city blocks.

Transparency

Their quick-growing nature and lightness of stem equips certain grasses such as some molinias, stipas and muhlenbergias to act as transparent or semi-transparent dividers of garden space. Excellent at providing height without weight in larger plantings—or in small gardens that are often short of space—these plants provide temporary division and something of an air of mystery as the view beyond can still be glimpsed behind the screen. The tall purple moor grass, *Molinia caerulea* subsp. *arundinacea*, is a great choice for cooler areas with its quite unique autumn display that sees the foliage, stems and flowerheads slowly turn the most amazing warm butter yellow—an ensemble that makes these plants the absolute stars at this time of year wherever they are used. *Stipa gigantea*, with its tall airy stems, is another good choice because although it can exceed 2 metres (6 feet), it can easily be used in front of much smaller plants at the front or middle areas of a border or larger planting area thanks to the 'see-through' nature of its flower stems.

Grassy Screening

The combination of regular outline, flower, movement and longevity allows a large number of grasses to be used very successfully as screens or hedges. They are just as easy to maintain when used as an informal hedge as they are in the garden border. Effectively self-levelling, the grasses grow to the same height each season without needing to be trimmed during the busy summer period.

A huge number of grasses can be used in this way and are superb in many situations where either a green or floriferous screen or hedge might be desirable. Unlike more permanent screening and commonly seen hedging plants, when used as lightweight 'hedging' grasses have few of the drawbacks of more traditional hedges, are long lived, and seldom become too bulky as the stems are renewed from the base each year. Although most grasses when grown together in this way produce a very even outline, the effect is generally informal rather in contrast to the strictly formal effect created by tightly clipped woody evergreens

Providing light and height is another useful attribute of taller grasses such as the panicum shown here, used as part of an entrance way planting to a retail nursery in Maryland. As well as providing height, colour and movement, the contrast between the solidity of the wooden building and the lightness of the grass is very satisfying as well as easy to maintain.

Height without undue weight is brought to this planting at Knoll Gardens through the use of *Molinia caerulea* subsp. *arundinacea* 'Karl Foerster'. Grasses with basal mounds of foliage and much taller stems and flowers such as the molinias and *Stipa gigantea* can create a transparent effect, imparting a sense of division and mystery without the need for heavyweight walling or hedging.

Partial division of space, while retaining a hint of what
lies beyond, can be achieved with grasses like *Calamagrostis ×acutiflora* 'Karl Foerster' as used so effectively on the waterside at Wilmington, Delaware.

such as box and yew. Added to this, the constant movement of stems, flowers and leaves brings the hedge alive.

Suitable candidates for informal hedging include the dwarf mounds of festucas, the comparatively short purple moor grass, *Molinia caerulea*, whose closely packed upright stems are quite superb as low-level hedges, and the mid-height *Pennisetum* 'Fairy Tails' whose unique upright habit is almost perfect for produced hedging in drier sunny soils. *Miscanthus sinensis* 'Abundance', aptly named for its freely flowering and compact habit, makes for one of the most floriferous of screens at mid height. Then there is the taller and much narrower feather reed grass, *Calamagrostis ×acutiflora* 'Karl Foerster', whose distinctive vertical stems are produced in such huge quantities on mature plants as to make this an almost perfect choice for taller screens. Taller still is the architectural *Miscanthus ×giganteus* whose strong green stems support gently cascading wide green leaves that shimmer and float all season. These grass hedges need trimming to ground level each spring, and so work best where temporary loss of the screen is not an issue.

FOUR
From Wild Grasslands to the Garden

Gras ist das Haar der Mutter Erde.

(Grass is the Hair of Mother Earth.)
— Karl Foerster

THE SAVANNAH OF Central Africa, the veldt of South Africa, the pampas of South America, the prairies of North America, the steppes of Asia and the meadows of Europe: all of these great grasslands exist (or used to) on a vast scale, covering square mile after square mile. Yet even when planning the smallest of domestic gardens, we can learn much from these great grasslands. Understanding how they are naturally composed, and tuning in to the spirit they evoke, can help us to imbue our own gardens with a pleasing sense of informality and longevity through the use of grasses.

The expansive meadow at Longwood Gardens, Pennsylvania is in fact a relatively recent (1969) creation, built on what was previously farmland. It perfectly captures a feeling of abundant growth and wide open space and provides a home for a rich diversity of animal, insect and plant life.

Drawing Inspiration from Prairies, Steppes and Meadows

To the casual eye, from a distance, these fabulous natural grasslands may look like monotonous (or even relentless) virtually uninterrupted expanses of 'just grass'. In reality this is far from the truth; like all successful communities, they are extremely diverse. The great grasslands evolved, sometimes in tandem with human civilization, to become distinctive ecosystems with their own specially adapted flora and fauna. Many so-called traditional garden plants have their roots in wild grasslands; poppies, those most beloved of garden flowers, hail from European meadows while golden rod, cone flowers and rudbeckias, which we have come to grow and love in our gardens, are denizens of the American prairie.

Roberto Burle Marx, the eminent Brazilian landscape designer, is credited with coining the phrase 'less is more'. Perhaps a natural grassland provides the perfect example of what this might mean for our designed spaces: a restrained palette of plants used in bold but sensitive ways can give an arresting feeling of place and space, of nature and of control. When seen in the wild, grasses' striking ability to define a mood and bring fluidity, movement and harmoniousness to a space explains why they work so well, on a smaller scale, in our designed gardens. It is precisely these qualities that our gardens so often sorely need.

On Evening Island at the Chicago Botanic Garden, the simple and refined use of a few well-chosen grasses on a massive scale is truly breathtaking. As the island's name suggests, the plantings where designers Wolfgang Oehme and James van Sweden have used *Miscanthus, Molinia* and *Panicum* are doubly effective each evening when low sunlight illuminates the countless grassy flowerheads. Here individual grasses are used in very large swathes. The garden is just one example of many successful ways in which we can draw inspiration from natural grasslands.

Grassland actually comes in all shapes and sizes, and can be found in many regions. The tall grass prairie is aptly named with much of the constituent plants growing to above head height. The grasses making up the European meadows and much of the steppes, on the other hand, are somewhat shorter. Thick, rough *Cortaderia* can make travel

This wonderful Oehme and van Sweden planting on Evening Island at the Chicago Botanic Garden borrows freely from the grassland ideal, using miscanthus to create seemingly endless flowing swathes through which thread numerous paths and trailways.

through South America's pampas anything but comfortable, and the savannah and many mediterranean grasslands close down during the heat of summer, going into dormancy until the essential life-giving rain arrives in autumn.

Acid, alkaline or serpentine; pure sand to solid clay; freezing cold or baking hot; dust-dry to distinctly wet: anywhere that has sufficient sunlight will mostly have its associated grassland community. And in no small measure it is this ability to survive and prosper under such a broad spectrum of conditions that makes grasses so desirable in our gardens.

The term 'meadow' has been applied to an area of predominantly grass (or grass-like plants) which without intervention, human or

High on Figueroa Mountain in California, a meadow of *Elymus elymoides* survives on an area of serpentine soil which the alien grasses, seen covering the background slopes and which were originally introduced to improve grazing, have difficulty penetrating.

otherwise, would eventually end up becoming woodland. This is known as being 'in transition', the natural process of moving from open ground to mature woodland. Contrastingly a true grassland is one where trees cannot grow due to one or more climatalogical factors such as lack of water, leading to more or less permanently open grassland.

A prairie is an example of a permanent grassland community (although apparently the word 'prairie', bestowed by early French travellers, actually means 'meadow' (according to Christopher Lloyd's *Meadows*). The word 'prairie' has become evocative of wide open spaces; more recently it has come to connote a style of planting which, in much of its detail, can bear little resemblance to the original. Being good for farming, huge tracts of prairie land in the United States have been converted to the extent that the term 'prairie remnant', used to describe what is left of these once-mighty grasslands, is now all too apt. These permanent grasslands have clearly not benefited from human intervention.

By contrast, Ferndown Common in Dorset, England is an example of an impermanent grassland that has benefited directly from human intervention. Although trees could thrive there, the area was cleared by early human activity of much of its tree cover sufficiently long ago for a specialized community of plants, including grasses, to have evolved, taking advantage of the open ground. Purple moor grass, *Molinia caerulea*, is now abundant but still relies on periodic human intervention to clear trees and scrub for its continued success.

How to Recreate the Grassland Spirit

From a gardener's viewpoint, while such name tags as prairie or meadow have some practical value for describing planting styles, these labels can be counterproductive if taken too literally or out of context. A true North American prairie is no more likely to feel at home in a European urban garden than an authentic English meadow will be happy in a mediterranean Californian backyard. Both types of grassland have evolved in response to a specific place and a given set of conditions; changing the place or the conditions inevitably affects the outcome. While an accurate recreation of a natural grassland, also sometimes known as a 'restoration', can have great merit (see Chapter Seven), it is really only practical in places that those individual communities once called home—so try not to have unrealistic expectations for your own grassy garden. Rather than trying to emulate every detail of natural grasslands, gardeners and designers should draw inspiration from their overall effect, feel and style.

Locally native purple moor grass, *Molinia caerulea*, creates a warm winter brown carpet in association with darker-coloured heathers and a background of pines, birch and oak on Ferndown Common in Dorset, England. The ancient demand for timber led to the felling of the forest, allowing the molinia to colonize the newly open spaces. Even today, such grasslands still rely on human intervention to prevent woody plants from claiming back lost territory.

THE BURNING QUESTION

Periodic wildfire has always been an essential feature of the natural grassland cycle; during hot, rainless summers the grass becomes tinder-dry and catches alight, clearing away tired old growth which allows vigorous new growth to start again. In managed areas of natural beauty, reserves and preserves, fire is something that must be contended with and planned for. Under relatively controlled conditions it is even an effective agricultural tool. But for domestic gardeners, of course, it is hardly a safe option—and for those gardening in drier parts of the world, the threat of fire can be a real issue, especially when domestic homes and gardens are in close proximity to areas that are part of a naturally occurring fire cycle.

Some gardeners in high-risk areas are taking steps to protect their gardens from the threat of fire. In mediterranean California, for example, the use of native *Aristida purpurea* as a meadow allowed to come close to the residence is part of a generally accepted design contingency to combat the threat of fire. Many grasses in mediterranean areas will go summer-dormant; without summer irrigation, they cease growth, turning brown until autumn rains come. (Some will even go summer-dormant regardless of how much water they are given.) Using summer-dormant grasses such as *A. purpurea* rather than woody plants for a given distance surrounding a house—the 'defensible area'—can help to reduce the amount of available fuel for a fire. In areas at risk of fire, trimming the grasses in midsummer, just before the highest threat of naturally occurring fire, can also help to reduce the danger.

In landscaping a private home in Monterey, California, Bernard Trainor used purple three awn with other native grasses to help anchor the site within the surrounding natural landscape. California native *Aristida purpurea* (right) has reddish purple flowers that gradually dry in the summer heat to a light beige-brown that visually links with the surrounding hillside (below). To reinforce this link, even some of the flanking walls are finished in a sympathetic colour (opposite top) and surrounded by the same mix of grasses, with an occasional non-native such as the taller purple *Calamagrostis ×acutiflora* 'Karl Foerster' for accent. The purple three awn is encouraged to come right up to the house, or at least to the parapet (opposite bottom).

THE GRASSLAND PRINCIPLE   Despite wildly varying local environments and prevailing conditions, all grassland communities owe their characteristic air—perhaps, indeed, their charisma—to their shared feature: a preponderance of grasses, with their characteristic linearity, in a generally open space. To evoke the spirit of natural grasslands in our own gardens, then, we should make grasses a key element of our planting design. But this is not to suggest that *only* grasses should be used in natural-grassland-inspired designs; while there is certainly enough shape, form, colour and contrast within the group to make a grasses-only planting very effective, in practice this style is more often seen in botanical establishments. One example is the impressive Grass Garden at London's Royal Botanic Gardens Kew, where the comprehensive collection has both an educational and a design ethic. In private gardens, contrastingly, I suggest following what I call the Grassland Principle: grasses should comprise twenty to eighty percent of the overall planting palette.

Look in detail and you will see that grassland composition is a mix of not only different grasses but also bulbs, annuals, perennials and woody plants. Grasses provide the basic layer (or 'matrix') but the other plants also have vital roles to play.

Woody plants provide structure, screening and colour from flowers, leaves and stems. Interest at a lower level comes from all manner of bulbous plants in the spring, followed by a plethora of different perennials, many originating from grasslands, such as *Rudbeckia*, *Echinacea*, *Helenium*, *Monarda* and *Aster* which provide a seasonally varying succession of colour and interest. All of this is framed and supported by the grass layer.

As Ferndown Common and its fabulous man-maintained grassland of *Molinia caerulea* is in fact only a few hundred yards from the garden at Knoll, we have drawn inspiration from it. Being native to the area, *Molinia* grows well in the sandy soils of the garden where we have used it as a base and a foil for other more solid companions such as the perennials *Eupatorium* 'Chocolate', *Echinacea purpurea* 'Ruby Giant' and *Sanguisorba officinalis* 'Pink Tanna'. Woody plants are represented by some dark green conifers, yew and viburnum which provide a backing and a screen from another part of the garden, while

early-season bulbs such as daffodils and camassia provide early colour before the grass has regrown. The whole area measures only about 25 square metres (30 square yards), excluding the backing woody plants, and while the molinia in this case makes up something like sixty per-cent of the actual area, its effects are counterbalanced by the larger perennials and the woody plants so that the border is far from being 'just grass'. Nonetheless, this grassland-inspired area, designed to work in harmony with the garden's conditions, has the effects of grassland: a distinctive linearity, a preponderance of grasses, the feeling of open space.

On a different scale, at Scampston Hall in Yorkshire, master designer Piet Oudolf has again used *Molinia caerulea*, this time in a selected form

While admittedly lacking more traditional flower early in the season, grass-only plantings can achieve a spectacular level of interest from high summer onwards—especially when many different grasses are used in the same area, as at the RHS Garden Wisley.

An excellent form of purple moor grass, *Molinia caerulea* subsp. *caerulea* 'Poul Petersen', is used to breathtaking effect at Scampston Hall, Yorkshire, in a modern interpretation of the grassland effect by master designer Piet Oudolf. Photograph courtesy of Alexandre Bailhache.

Molinia caerulea subsp. *caerulea* 'Poul Petersen', in a design that blends a grassland approach with the formality often encountered in more traditional larger gardens. While the individual beds are one hundred percent molinia, this is balanced by other more formal elements such as lawn grass and hedging, greatly reducing the percentage of actual ground covered by the molinia. Although very formal in layout, much of the design's 'wow' factor comes from the simple use of a native grass planted in large quantities.

It is easy to understand how the Grassland Principle works by looking at larger areas like Scampston Hall and Evening Island at Chicago Botanic Gardens, where grasses are used in bold swathes to cover significant areas of ground. But can the Grasslands Principle work in much smaller spaces? The answer is a simple 'yes'.

Our gardens are typically composed of a varying mixture of borders, hedging, pathways and lawns. On a larger scale, each of these different areas is big enough to work well on its own. But on a more diminutive scale, borders are often too small to contain any depth of planting, lawns simply cumbersome to cut and too small to be useable, and shrubs and hedges sometimes clipped into formless and deeply uninteresting shapes. In other words, dividing a small outdoor space into separate sections often means that the whole area risks becoming virtually worthless; we expend time, energy and precious resources on something that gives little pleasure or even basic satisfaction. A new approach is needed, and adopting the Grassland Principle provides the practical solution.

Rather than focusing on its subdivisions—borders, hedging, pathways, lawn—think of the small garden as a single area that has several different jobs to do. Merge the lawn space with the border area using a basic ground layer of grasses and a mulch layer through which can come all sorts of plants from early spring bulbs to floriferous perennials and woody shrubs to provide permanent shape and screening. We readily carpet or otherwise cover the floors of our interior living spaces, mostly in a similar single material, from wall to wall—and there is little reason not to do the same outdoors. Pathways can simply be spaces left between the plants, and sitting areas can be almost anywhere and moved as the garden changes. Not only will the same area be much easier to maintain, but it will also be of significantly greater value to wildlife, and infinitely more pleasing to the gardener.

THE GRASSLAND PRINCIPLE IN PRACTICE

- Grasses should comprise 20–80% of the total number of plants used in the garden mix. If selected carefully, a higher percentage (50% or more) can provide the greatest 'wow' factor, strongly evoking the spirit of grassy meadows or prairies. A lower percentage of grasses is useful as a theme or backing to other plantings such as with perennials.
- When using a higher percentage of grasses, choose a restrained palette of 1–5 different grasses as a basic mix or ground covering. A larger number of different grasses can subsequently be used as accents or highlights of the remaining planting. (However, more than 5 species of *Carex* may be used together as a ground pattern as their overall shape can be quite similar.)
- Avoid using too few specimens of the same plant in one place. Grasses almost always work best when planted in larger numbers, whether placed as a drift meandering through a grassy space or en masse as part of a larger planting.
- Go large. Make the planting area as big as possible; the larger the area, the greater the grasses' effect. Small borders are always more work and less effective. Merge smaller borders with lawns to make more planting space.
- Pathways and sitting areas should be an integral part of the planting, rather than separate from it. For low-use pathways, simply leave sufficient space between the plants for people to walk through. Using a similar material as surface mulch for the planting areas and the walkways gives a great sense of space and is easier to install.
- Woody plants and perennials are essential to most successful plantings. Choose woody plants for year-round effect, bark and leaf colour and for permanent screening. Choose perennials that provide flower colour and form, ideally those that maintain their shape after flowering to provide long-term contrast with grasses. Such

perennials include *Echinacea, Eupatorium, Persicaria, Rudbeckia* and *Sedum.*

• All manner of bulbous plants can be used to provide early-season colour, especially with deciduous grasses which are at their least interesting in the spring. Bulbs are usually added in the autumn wherever a space is suitable.

• Prepare the ground before planting. Grasses are no different from other garden plants in that reasonable soil conditions will ensure best growth and establishment. However, unlike many garden plants, grasses do not need much fertilizer or water once established. Ensuring that the ground is not compacted and laying a surface mulch after planting are perhaps the two most important elements of preparation.

TOP CHOICES FOR A GRASSLAND OR MEADOW EFFECT

The following grasses are tried and tested for evoking the spirit of wild grassland or a naturalistic meadow in the garden.

Aristida purpurea
Bouteloua, most species
Briza media and its forms
Carex, especially good for shade and damp: most species, including *C. praegracilis, C. remota* and *C. divulsa*
Deschampsia, especially *D. cespitosa* for damp
Eragrostis, most species but especially *E. curvula, E. trichodes* and *E. spectabilis*
Festuca, nearly all good for sun and well-drained soil
Molinia caerulea, which tolerates wet and dry conditions
Nassella, most species
Panicum virgatum and forms
Pennisetum, most species and forms
Stipa, most species and forms

FIVE

Reinventing the Classic Plant Border: A Naturalistic Experiment

ABOUT SEVEN YEARS ago I found myself faced with the task of planning and replanting a large border at Knoll. The team and I wanted to create something exciting that would be effective over a long period. But at the same time, we knew that we would lack the resources to maintain a strictly traditional border on so large a scale.

A classic garden border, where plants are grown closely together, is usually edged by pathways, hedges, driveways or lawns which mark a distinct division of space and purpose. When done well, tightly controlled borders that rely on relatively regimented planting can create displays of enormous beauty and are superb examples of horticultural flair and ability. But they can also require an amazing amount of time and attention, so that deadheading, staking, tying, spraying and even successional planting are regular parts of the summer workload. Failure

With the pampas in full bloom (centre left) and supported by swiftly colouring woody plants such as the spindle trees, *Euonymus europaeus*, which contribute brightly coloured fruits as well as leaves, the Decennium border is possibly at its most resplendent in September and October, although its interest is maintained virtually year-round.

to keep up with these processes usually results in the decline and eventual failure of the border itself.

A longtime admirer of what has been termed the modern European style of planting, spearheaded by such eminent designers as Piet Oudolf from Holland, I had been especially struck by the imaginative Hermannshof Garden in Weinheim, Germany. I liked how the generous use of grasses allowed for a greater concentration on late summer and autumn, rather than the more traditional spring and early summer. And their use of permanent planting to achieve a series of successional highs of colour and interest seemed an irresistibly common-sense approach. The team and I were keen to incorporate elements of this style in the new planting.

The new border became known as Decennium (meaning 'ten years'; it was created in our tenth year at Knoll). It was something of an experiment, as new as it was exciting. Having spent some time selecting the plants that I hoped would achieve that all-important succession of interest throughout the year, I was nervous that obvious gaps would appear in the display if I had gotten things wrong. But very soon after the initial planting, the border began to prove its worth as the plants grew and the limited palette seemed to work well together. Now it is a favourite area of the garden, both for myself and for visitors; it has something to offer virtually every week throughout the entire year.

Moving Away from Traditional Constraints

The Decennium border was intended to incorporate elements of the naturalistic style, with a more relaxed, informal and low-maintenance approach to planting. As such, it represented a marked departure from more traditional thinking about border and flowerbed plantings.

FROM SUCCESSIONAL PLANTING TO 'RIGHT PLANT, RIGHT PLACE' In the past, especially in larger gardens and parks where space and labour allowed, different areas or borders were often designed for certain seasons: one area for spring, a border for summer and so on so that the gardens offered a succession of interest throughout the year. Less interesting parts of the garden were simply ignored in favour of the areas currently looking their best. But with the number of domestic private gardens growing larger and their average size becoming smaller, it is not always practical or desirable to dedicate a border to each season; borders now must work much harder at providing that much-sought-after successional interest. More is being demanded from less space.

Accordingly, in more recent years successional planting has come to describe the practice of replacing plants that have gone over with others that are fresh and new as seasons change. This can be an almost continuous process. Once the skill is learned, the technique works well—but it requires a level of work and commitment that is too onerous for many gardeners.

The 'new wave' style of planting, contrastingly, requires not only choosing the right plant for the right place but also carries the added discipline of selecting plants that can provide different levels of interest, in combination with others, over a long period. And the plants selected should be able to perform without being deadheaded, staked or otherwise fussed over. In light of these requirements, the list of suitable plants is constantly being refined. In the Decennium border, we tried to choose plants that would thrive in the garden's condition and give optimal value year-round.

A SOFTENING OF BOUNDARIES   Highly formal, traditional borders rely on accurate placing of individual plants in relation to their neighbours as well as the boundaries of the border. Indeed it is often the relationship between plants and the border's edges, especially paths and lawns, that is most problematic. Plant too close to the edge and constant cutting back is needed; plant too far back and the soil needs covering or otherwise keeping free from weeds.

Removing any clear division between border and pathway at the design stage avoids these maintenance issues while also giving a more natural free-flowing look to the overall design. When any hard division is deliberately obscured or removed, the area becomes easier to plant successfully. The maintenance burden is reduced as the planting area's edges are softened and the aesthetic becomes more informal.

Our new 'border' actually encompassed two pathways as well as an open space underneath the canopy of a pine which was intended to become an accessible area with seating. (While grasses may not be generally keen on the driest shade, garden visitors were known to enjoy such places, especially on sunny days.) To link everything together, creating an informal free-flowing planting, not only did the planting pattern have to be repeated but the surfaces of the pathways and planted areas needed to be covered in the same material. During preparation the paths were in fact clearly marked out to make sure they were wide and firm enough, but no distinct edges were created so that once planted and covered in the same material used under the plants, such as chipped bark, the pathways would simply appear as informal spaces between the plantings.

Building the Decennium Border at Knoll

The area to be planted had just been cleared of an ailing collection of closely planted conifers. These trees had once contributed a central circular feature of some substance, but had become rather tired after almost thirty years in the ground. One magnificent pine remained; it was really too good to remove, and there was a concern about too large a void appearing in the very centre of the garden. So it remained to give some height and a feeling of maturity to what was otherwise going to be a very new planting. However, gardening often involves compromises and this remaining tree would limit the choice of plants that could be used under its canopy and within reach of its roots.

Our garden soil was almost entirely free-draining and sand-like—easy to work, but prone to losing moisture almost instantly and with a comparatively low rainfall. At only 20 metres (60 ft.) above sea level it was in something of a local frost pocket, and while most of the border was in open sun there were also substantial areas of shade.

Preparation consisted of mechanically removing the old conifer stumps and thoroughly digging over the soil using a hydraulically operated toothed digging bucket. The soil was re-levelled to create a gently undulating surface, lightly rotovated and finally raked level in readiness for planting. No organic matter or fertilizer was added.

PLANTING FOR YEAR-ROUND INTEREST   The mere inclusion of grasses, especially the deciduous group, can extend the length of time a planting makes an impact; grasses are often at their peak in the second half of the year, with many still making an effective contribution into the following spring. Many traditional perennial border plants are grown primarily for their flower contribution and lack this longevity of display. By mixing perennials with grasses, a border's period of usefulness can be significantly extended. Further thoughtful selection of grasses and perennials, chosen specifically for their ability to work together over a long period of time, can produce borders whose season of display lasts longer than ten months of the year.

Working with a limited and refined plant palette allows for repeated use of the same groups of plants throughout the border. This repetition has the added bonus of developing a unifying theme and a feeling of depth, especially if the border can be viewed from different directions.

In the Decennium border, grasses account for around sixty percent of the total number of plants used in the whole planting. Being mostly composed of deciduous plants, the border is cut to the ground in late March or early April. Then follows its 'down time' of a few short weeks before the plants re-awaken into active growth. This is a convenient period for any annual maintenance, replanting or weeding that might be needed. But even during this period the evergreen (and so uncut) *Anemanthele lessoniana* (or *Stipa arundinacea* as it was known until recently) makes an effective contribution under the canopy of the pine or in the shadow of the larger boundary shrubs. The pheasant grass is accompanied by the delicate-looking flowers of *Pulsatilla vulgaris* which, while only a few inches tall, are a welcome sign of the seasonal procession that is only just starting.

Just a few weeks later, often by the end of April, the spurge, *Euphorbia palustris*, has achieved a speed of growth that allows it to display its bright acid-yellow bracts set off perfectly by the bright green foliage of emerging grasses and other perennials.

Before long, the first deep red poppy flowers from *Papaver orientale* (Goliath Group) 'Beauty of Livermere' appear as if from nowhere at various points through the border to link with the bright yellow of the spurge in a symphony of bright spring colours that is only enhanced with the arrival of the locally native white daisy, *Leucanthemum vulgare*.

As the euphorbia fades into its summer dress its place is taken by the amazing whorled spikes of Jerusalem sage, *Phlomis russeliana*, whose large heart-shaped leaves provide a striking foil to so many other plants for so long a period. The lavender-mauve upright fingers of *Veronicastrum virginicum* contrast beautifully with the various yellows, as does the spiky upright-stemmed but darker purple *Verbena bonariensis*, which later still will have the tall bright yellow flowers of *Rudbeckia laciniata* with which to partner.

All the while, the grasses such as *Miscanthus*, *Molinia* and *Pennisetum* are creating ever-taller mounds of linear foliage that move easily in the lightest wind and provide a perfect backdrop to these earlier-season perennials. *Calamagrostis ×acutiflora* 'Karl Foerster' is already showing its strongly upright habit with fresh flower that is yet to turn its trademark buff and brown. The soft grey leaves and stems of *Panicum virgatum* 'Heavy Metal', still not at full height, provide a more solid backdrop to the red, rounded heads of *Sanguisorba officinalis* which are so light and airy that they appear almost disconnected from the ground.

High summer sees the arrival of the large flat heads of Joe Pye weed or *Eupatorium maculatum* Atropurpureum Group in the highest parts of the border while the cone flower, *Echinacea purpurea* 'Leuchtstern', delights with its range of shorter but no less stunning flowers.

Finally the main season grasses, now at full height and shape, make their presence truly felt as masses of fresh flowers emerge from hitherto green stems. The dark red of *Miscanthus sinensis* 'Ferner Osten' and the pendulous rich pink of *Miscanthus sinensis* 'Flamingo' are both stunning on their own or in concert with others. The panicums, characteristic in flower, provide masses of tiny flowers that create cloud-like effects through which other more solid companions can seem to float.

For some time *Pennisetum alopecuroides* 'Hameln' will have contributed dark green leaves in an easily distinguishable rounded outline. Now is the moment to understand why pennisetums are called fountain grasses; the flowers appear virtually without warning, and in such quantity that they really resemble fountains.

As high summer turns almost imperceptibly into early autumn, the subtle colourations of the grasses turn if anything more intense. The fresh flower colour fades, but is replaced with more understated tones that capture the spirit of the season: smoky fall colours that are rich in oranges, yellows and reds and that seem to change daily.

The tall *Molinia caerulea* subsp. *arundinacea* 'Karl Foerster' has remained almost in a background role until, as the summer colour starts to ebb away, the stems, flowers and leaves all turn the most intense butter yellow. The delicate tracery of its gently curving stems and flowers provide an essay on colour and form that is complete in itself.

Between November and Christmas, the last of the autumnal colour fades and is replaced by even more subtle variations in beiges and browns. Far from being uniform, the diversity of outline, colour and texture of the different grasses and perennials provides yet another level of interest and contrast that is only sharpened and enhanced by winter frost and low-level sunlight. The ability of the grasses and their accompanying perennials to stand through the winter, providing displays of delicate beauty whenever encouraged by frost or sunny days, endows the border with value and interest for the longest possible period: right through to early spring, when the gradually lengthening days herald the start of yet another repeat performance.

PLANTING PALETTE FOR THE DECENNIUM BORDER

Grasses	Perennials
Anemanthele lessoniana	*Echinacea purpurea* 'Leuchtstern'
Calamagrostis ×*acutiflora* 'Karl Foerster'	*Eupatorium maculatum* Atropurpureum Group
Miscanthus sinensis 'Abundance'	*Euphorbia palustris*
Miscanthus sinensis 'Ferner Osten'	*Leucanthemum vulgare*
Miscanthus sinensis 'Flamingo'	*Papaver orientale* (Goliath Group) 'Beauty of Livermere'
Miscanthus sinensis 'Little Kitten'	*Phlomis russelliana*
Molinia caerulea	*Rudbeckia laciniata*
Molinia caerulea subsp. *arundinacea* 'Karl Foerster'	*Sanguisorba officinalis*
Panicum virgatum 'Hänse Herms'	*Verbena bonariensis*
Panicum virgatum 'Heavy Metal'	*Veronicastrum virginicum*
Pennisetum alopecuroides 'Hameln'	

For the first few weeks after being cut back in late March, the border
is at its least interesting. This is the annual opportunity to take stock,
to replant, to divide, to weed and to mulch before the ground is
quickly covered again by the season's first flush of new growth.

Although the major groups of plants are only starting to regrow after their annual cut down (above), March and early April see the wind flowers, *Pulsatilla vulgaris* (left), contribute the first of the season's long display of interest with their delicate-looking flowers in many shade of pinks, blues, mauves and whites.

As April slips into May (above), the border begins its period of rapid growth. While grasses such as *Calamagrostis ×acutiflora* 'Karl Foerster', to the left of the border, have produced sheafs of new foliage, the large heart-shaped leaves of *Phlomis russeliana* in the foreground have already made wonderful ground cover, setting off the bright acid yellow flowers of *Euphorbia palustris* which recovers and flowers in an amazingly short space of time; strong young shoots produce their first flowers only a few weeks after the euphorbia is cut down.

By early June (right) the euphorbia's strong yellow is joined by the strong blowsy red of *Papaver orientale* (Goliath Group) 'Beauty of Livermere' and the small white daisy flowers of *Leucanthemum vulgare*.

As spring yellows fade in mid June (above) they are replaced by softer whites, from the locally native daisy, *Leucanthemum vulgare*, and the rather more bulky *Periscaria polymorpha*. To the left the first spiky purples, belonging to *Veronicastrum virginicum* as well as an occasional foxglove, are beginning to show.

Veronicastrum virginicum (left) is one of many easy-growing perennials with distinct shape and form that work so well among grasses.

By August (above) the border is reaching a peak of flower colour. Fennel and verbena partner with *Miscanthus sinensis* 'Ferner Osten' which boasts one of the darkest red flowers of any miscanthus. In the central background, the massed spikes of a pampas, *Cortaderia selloana* 'Sunningdale Silver', are about to open.

On the other side of the verbena and miscanthus (right), the fluffy cylindrical flowers of *Pennisetum alopecuroides* 'Hameln' are joining the pink cone flowers of *Echinacea purpurea* 'Leuchtstern' which have been in flower already for some weeks. Backing the cone flowers is the soft hazy foliage and flower of *Panicum virgatum* 'Hänse Herms', and behind the panicum is an uninvited seedling of the poke weed, *Phytolacca americana*—placing itself, with an eye for design, perfectly between less solid companions.

A pathway (above) meanders unhurriedly through the planting, linking two otherwise separate areas of lawn. With the same bark surface used for both path and border mulch, the path is defined only by the shapes of the plants which alter as the season progresses.

In late September (left), as the light lowers and takes on that special autumn quality, the border is arguably at its most beautiful. The textural quality of the miscanthus and the golden yellow transparency of the molinia combine with the fall foliage red of zelkova, the yellow of the birch and the darkness of the evergreen pine to create a complete picture that captures the very essence of the season.

Soft light on a dew-laden
autumn morning (above)
can create memorable effects.
Here the fluffy caterpillar-
like flowers of *Pennisetum
alopecuroides* 'Hameln' seem
to double in size and inten-
sity when covered in dew.

Clear light on a frosty December morning (right) illuminates groups of *Panicum virgatum* 'Heavy Metal' and
Miscanthus sinensis 'Flamingo'
along with the darker brown
stems, leaves and heads of
Eupatorium maculatum Atropurpureum Group and *Veronicastrum virginicum*—creating
a display of delicate beauty to
rival that of any other season.

During the first few days of February (above), a fresh covering of snow acts as a perfect foil for the grasses, turning their dried skeletal stems a warm brown. At the front the lollipop-like structures are seedheads of *Phlomis russeliana*, each delicately topped with its own covering of snow.

Further snowfall in February (left) dramatically demonstrates the insulation capabilities of a tree canopy. While the rest of the border is weighed down by snow, the group of *Anemanthele lessoniana* stays protected in its own virtual island created by the canopy of the large pine overhead. The constantly dropping pine needles make a self-renewing surface mulch surrounding the tree.

SIX

Right Grass, Right Place

Design sets down the basic forms but soon the garden
is in nature's grip. Then, with careful nurturing, the
garden's performance will outshine your imagination.
—Wolfgang Oehme and James van Sweden
Bold Romantic Gardens

PLANTS ARE HAPPIEST, and therefore easiest to look after, when growing under conditions they enjoy or at least easily tolerate. A thoughtful
look at the established plant communities in natural systems shows us
that plants arrange themselves into areas that best suit their needs or to
which they have become adapted. Over time, a process of natural selection matches the right plant to the right place.

In our gardens this natural process is interrupted and replaced with
a variety of other considerations that can have very little, if anything at
all, to do with matching plant with place. However, the more we can
understand our gardens' basic growing conditions, the better we will

On the beach at Poole, Dorset, England, the
native lyme grass, *Leymus arenarius*, must cope
with a combination of full sun, reflected heat
from the sand, frequent drying winds and
ultra-dry, continually shifting ground.

be able to match the most suitable plants with those conditions, and so the better our gardens will be.

Easy as they are, grasses have their likes and dislikes, their preferences as to position and soil—all based on where they come from in nature. Luckily for gardeners, a huge number of grasses are actually quite happy in a wide range of average garden conditions. However, in this chapter we will look at some of the more challenging environments that can be found in gardens, exploring which grasses might be best suited to these conditions.

Grasses for Sun-baked, Gravel and Drought Situations

By far the greatest number of grasses come from open and sunny, if not outrightly dry and drought-prone, natural areas—so there is a very large number of grasses from which to choose for varying degrees of dryness and drought.

Whether on a beach in the constantly shifting sand dunes of mild maritime climates or in the harsher conditions of more arid, desert-like areas, drought and sun-baked conditions involve a shortage of water for at least part of the year. Combined with high summer temperatures, drying winds and often gravelly well-drained soils, such conditions will literally 'cook' or 'fry' all but the most resilient of plants.

Under drought conditions most plants, especially those with large leaves such as hostas and ligularias, will show signs of short-term stress by visibly wilting. Grasses can be tough customers under such short-term stress, appearing hardly to notice the lack of moisture, though many will eventually roll or curl their leaves so that they present less surface area to the daytime sun until sufficient moisture returns. For grasses that have specialized in extreme conditions like the beach grasses—the marram, *Ammophila*, or wild rye, *Leymus*—adaptations such as tough waxy leaves and a questing root system allow them to survive and indeed thrive where few others can follow. Where prolonged summer droughts are a regular feature, such as in mediterranean areas, many grasses including *Aristida*, *Bouteloua*, *Melica* and

Nassella in common with other regionally adapted plants will go into summer dormancy, shutting down active growth during the hottest and driest months of the year and then starting back into growth with the arrival of the autumn rains. In drier desert-like conditions where water is an unreliable and occasional luxury, grasses will remain in active growth only while there is sufficient moisture in the ground.

For the gardener, such drought-adapted qualities can also be marked out by the presence of grey or blue foliage. *Elymus*, *Festuca*, *Helictotrichon*, *Leymus*, *Poa* and *Sesleria* are all drought-tolerant grasses that have the signature blue-tinted foliage which has a very ornamental quality much prized by gardeners and can be grown easily in most sunny dry soils. For warmer climates *Leymus condensatus*, especially in its superb form *L. condensatus* 'Canyon Prince', is perhaps unrivalled for providing strong mounds of comparatively wide icy blue foliage especially when topped by its magnificent flowers, while for less favoured areas *Leymus arenarius* will contribute something similar though on a lesser scale.

On a smaller scale again, *Helictotrichon sempervirens* is a wonderful clump-forming 'blue' that forms a very attractive rounded outline composed of stiff leaves that make a distinctive contribution wherever it is used. Even smaller, *Festuca* is a very wide and adaptable family with almost-hair-like narrow leaves that offers perhaps the greatest number of different cultivars including those deriving from *Festuca glauca*. Of these, *Festuca glauca* 'Elijah Blue' is perhaps one of the most reliable performers. As all festucas seed readily it is important to choose cultivated selections from a reliable source as so often inferior seedlings have become mixed with the original cultivar material. The widespread and highly adaptable *Festuca rubra* has some wonderful offerings including the steely blue-grey of *F.* 'Molate Blue' and the lighter blue-grey of *F.* 'Patrick's Point'. Smaller still, and definitely underused, is *Sesleria caerulea* whose tight mounds of evergreen bicoloured green and blue-grey leaves are tough and durable even in some shade in warmer areas.

Garden conditions in urban areas can present a similar set of challenges, whether in small domestic gardens, on roof terraces or even in

In the relatively cool conditions of Arroyo Grande,
California, a gravel pathway
meanders through infor-
mal plantings including
Carex testacea, *Festuca* and
Helictotrichon, in the garden
of Dave and Rainie Fross.

those areas that surround commercial buildings or public areas in our
towns and cities. Growing conditions in these places can be just as trying for plants as in any natural environment. The combination of hard
paved areas such as roads, parking areas, roofs and walls all contribute
to the creation of heat islands; heat from the sun, from buildings and
from vehicles is reflected and radiated by the hard surfaces which at the
same time prevent much-needed water from reaching and replenishing
the ground, redirecting it through storm drains away from where it is
perhaps most needed. The result is a continually warm environment
that is short on water (for all intents and purposes, a desert).

Well known for its hot, dry, desert location, Las Vegas, Nevada
uses drought-adapted grasses to great effect. From the stunning pink

muhly, *Muhlenbergia capillaris*, in the car park (parking lot) of the unique Springs Reserve to *Pennisetum* 'Fairy Tails' surrounding an upscale shopping mall, a simple but refined palette of grasses provide an effective, visually pleasing solution to hot, dry environments.

Other members of the beautiful muhly family include *Muhlenbergia rigens* with its immediately distinctive outline and *M. rigida* whose seductive pink flowers are especially vibrant in the form 'Nashville'. Both tolerate hot dry conditions, as does *M. lindheimeri* and others such as the quite unique bamboo muhly, *M. dumosa*. Coming from warm desert-like areas, the bamboo muhly has insignificant tiny yellow flowers but its bamboo-like woody stems and leaves place it firmly in the top flight of all foliage plants. Revelling in hot mediterranean-type

In this motel garden in Monterey, California, clearly rounded but spiky foliage of *Helictotrichon sempervirens* contrasts with rock, slab, bark and building. Blue-tinted foliage is mostly an adaptation for sunny drought-prone areas; the colouring becomes more pronounced the more extreme the conditions.

This simple but highly effective planting of palms and drought-resistant grasses in Las Vegas, Nevada clearly demonstrates that aesthetics and utility can be combined to create harmonious partnerships.

climates, the bamboo muhly's adaptability allows it to grow successfully in much less favoured localities such as at RBG Kew, London, in the ground and also at Knoll Gardens in Dorset where in pots it survives temperatures colder than −8°C (18°F) in winter.

All fountain grasses, members of the *Pennisetum* family, revel in hot, high-sunshine areas to the extent that all demand excellent drainage and sun to grow successfully in gardens. Although the seeding potential of some such as *Pennisetum setaceum* is an issue in sensitive areas, there are some excellent gardenworthy forms for easy use in all other areas. Pinks and whites are the flower colours favoured by fountain grasses, and produced in such profusion it is difficult not to be impressed by them. With one or two exceptions, such as *P.* ×*advena* 'Rubrum' whose purple

foliage and long arching flowers are exquisite but only hardy in warmer areas, the foliage of fountains is not very exciting. *Pennisetum villosum* has large, fluffy caterpillar-like white flowers that literally cascade down the light green foliage when in full flower, amply demonstrating how the common name arose. Although perhaps the least hardy of the commonly grown fountains, it will grow in most areas as long as it has excellent drainage. *Pennisetum orientale* has a little less vigour but produces a large number of delicate pink flowers in a noticeably rounded outline and is the parent of several different very worthwhile hybrids and cultivars such as the rather taller and upright *P. o.* 'Karley Rose', whose flowers are a comparatively strong pink, and *P. o.* 'Shogun' with slightly softer pink flowers set off perfectly by the grey-green leaves.

When used close to buildings, large, simple blocks of grasses offer lightness and movement in clear contrast to impassive solidity. At a shopping mall in Las Vegas, *Pennisetum* 'Fairy Tails' provides an almost perfect antidote to the overabundance of hard surfaces.

Urban conditions, with a high percentage of paving and other hard surfaces, create 'heat islands' that reflect light and heat while repelling water, and can be very harsh on plants, especially in warmer climates. Fountain grasses such as *Pennisetum ×advena* 'Rubrum' are better adapted to such extremes and make excellent practical choices under such conditions.

Pennisetum alopecuroides has given rise to many very worthwhile garden cultivars, so that while the species itself can produce poor levels of flower in cooler and more maritime climates the cultivars will perform admirably on sunny, well-drained soils. *Pennisetum alopecuroides* 'Hameln' is perhaps one of the oldest but very useful for its distinct rounded outline of foliage that is quite literally covered in smaller but generously produced flowers. *Pennisetum alopecuroides* 'Red Head' is a recent form that has large dark flowers that are initially quite red at first while *Pennisetum* 'Dark Desire' has amazingly large dark to almost-black cylindrical heads of flower that demand attention.

While aridity and dryness are major limiting factors in warm

climates, those areas which have the benefit of higher rainfall and cooler summer temperatures may regard such limitations as advantages. Dry, well-drained soils that provide comparatively dry conditions for roots during an otherwise wet and cold winter period will frequently make the difference between success and failure for many plants, including sun-loving grasses that are accustomed to warmer, drier environments. *Bouteloua*, *Bothriochloa*, *Eragrostis*, *Jarava*, *Muhlenbergia*, *Pennisetum* and *Stipa* are just some of the grasses that revel in relatively hot dry and sunny conditions but can be grown successfully in cooler, more mild climates if given full sun exposure and well-drained soils.

For example, although the garden at Knoll is in southern England it

These brown grasses are in fact sedges, *Carex* species, that have a relatively short life span, at least under garden conditions. At the frequently dry and windswept RHS Garden Hyde Hall in Essex, England, the originally planted *Carex comans* specimens have long since died, to be replaced by seedlings that have been allowed to gradually colonize, creating this satisfyingly natural-looking planting.

At Knoll Gardens, the gravel garden is sited on dry sandy soil that is frequently short of moisture, allowing dry-loving grasses like *Pennisetum macrourum* (front left), *Muhlenbergia rigens* (centre) and *Miscanthus nepalensis* (far right) to thrive. Photograph courtesy of Dianna Jazwinski.

forms part of a local frost pocket, with poor air drainage—and at just 20 metres (60 ft.) above sea level, it will record temperatures at least as low as −12°C (10°F) each winter. However, as the garden consists almost exclusively of a very fine sandy soil, most of the soil and therefore the plants' roots are comparatively dry during these low temperatures. A combination of moisture and low temperatures causes the majority of damage to plants, so having a soil that remains comparatively dry during the winter allows us to grow many plants including grasses that might not otherwise survive. We can therefore enjoy the bright pink flowers of *Bothriochloa bladhii*, the amazing cascade of narrow flower spikes from *Muhlenbergia rigens*, the gold, braid-like nodding flowers of the unequalled *Miscanthus nepalensis* and the simply stunning masses

of white flowers produced by *Jarava ichu* (formerly *Stipa ichu*) with only the occasional losses in more exceptional circumstances.

In heavier soils the addition of grit and gravels is often recommended to open up and improve the drainage and to help dry out the soil. However, a far more satisfactory technique is to raise the planting area by adding soil and organic matter, or to reshape and re-grade, to provide a planting area that is at least 15 cm (6 in.) or so above the surrounding area. This will allow the moisture to drain away from the roots and crowns of the plants which will considerably enhance the chances of successful cultivation.

Gravel gardens are popular and practical in dry areas that are mostly open to full sun. On a basic level they consist of a decorative layer of

Gravel can be a practical, effective and longlasting substitute for lawn grass, especially useful in areas where the amount of water used to maintain such a sward would be considered environmentally unsound. The shaggy outline of groups of deer grass, *Muhlenbergia rigens*, provides a fine contrast in shape and form to the relative flatness of the surrounding surface, even before flowering begins.

Beth Chatto's Gravel Garden in Essex, England combines aesthetics with horticultural experiment. In an already low-rainfall area, and on dry gravelly soils, this area is never irrigated; the chosen plants must survive whatever the prevailing weather conditions offer. Reed, hair, oat and silver spear grasses all appear to thrive in the testing conditions.

gravel, or other similar natural stone material, extended to cover the surface of an area through which plants are grown. The depth can vary from 2.5 to 7.5 cm (1–3 in.) and it works well on relatively large areas as a cost-effective substitute for high-maintenence turf grass or other high-water-use plantings. Using an ornamental finish in this way can allow for greater spacing between individuals and groups of plants than would otherwise be acceptable.

On another level, gravel gardens combine free-draining soils, full sun exposure and low rainfall with drought-tolerant plants, drawing inspiration from naturally occurring drought-prone communities. For example, Beth Chatto's famous Gravel Garden in Essex, England is described as a horticultural experiment; based on dry, poor soils in an already dry, low-rainfall area, the plants have been chosen for their ability to withstand prolonged periods of drought as this part of the garden is never watered. Even in these very dry conditions, *Achnatherum calamagrostis* (formerly *Stipa calamagrostis*), *Stipa gigantea*, *Nassella tenuissima* and even *Calamagrostis* such as *C. ×acutiflora* 'Karl Foerster' all thrive—and are arguably at their best when conditions are driest.

Attention to the surface detail can add greatly to the aesthetic value of the mulch. While evenly sized gravel is most common, using different sizes of material, from small thimble sizes through to comparatively large boulders, creates an extra level of interest. The use of locally sourced materials can add significantly to the sense of place, helping to relate the garden to the surrounding wider environment. A further refinement of this style involves the use of reclaimed materials such as crushed brick or rubble, which provide an excellent foil for plants as well as serving as a practical mulch while also re-using existing materials.

Summer dormancy in arid climates is an entirely natural response to prevailing conditions, just as winter dormancy is in colder areas. While summer dormancy is perhaps something of an acquired taste for gardeners accustomed to greener summer landscapes, it is an acceptable aesthetic in its own right. Allowing grasses and other plants to follow their customary natural pattern under garden situations offers a more genuine approach to truly sustainable gardening that links the right plant with the right place. The Strybing Arboretum in San Francisco, and the Leaning Pine Arboretum in San Luis Obispo, both in California, maintain good summer-dormant gardens that are as aesthetically pleasing in the height of summer as they are during any other season.

Under controlled garden conditions water is frequently available through irrigation, though the indiscriminate use of this finite and precious resource is increasingly, and correctly, coming into question. Even under the most arid of conditions, using drought-adapted grasses can significantly reduce the quantity and regularity of additional water that is needed to keep the plants alive. Embracing summer dormancy as an acceptable, even desirable, aesthetic in areas where it is a natural occurrence seems a highly sensible way to conserve water in places where it is already most precious.

In a meadow setting at the San Francisco Botanical Society's Garden in the Strybing Arboretum, a collection of native grasses clearly demonstrates the beauty and utility of summer dormancy in mediterranean climates. Photograph courtesy of Dave Fross.

Truly summer-dormant grasses, such as the needle grasses, *Nassella*, can find it hard to adapt to conditions where a plentiful supply of water avoids the necessity of a summer closedown. *Nassella cernua, N. lepida* and *N. pulchra* are all exceptionally beautiful when in green and active growth but offer just as much, if in a more restrained way, in their dried state. For such highly adapted grasses, excessive summer moisture can indeed have deadly consequences. Contrastingly plants like the alkali sacaton, *Sporobolus airoides*, are quite beautiful if allowed to go into summer dormancy but can also tolerate summer water quite easily, so that they can be used along with other plants that require some summer water.

Nassella tenuissima (formerly *Stipa tenuissima*) is a quick-growing, easy-to-please evergreen producing dense heads of beige flowers and revelling in dry sunny conditions. Moving in the slightest breeze, especially when in full flower, it is perfect for this public park planting in frequently windy San Francisco.

TOP CHOICES FOR SUN-BAKED, GRAVEL AND DROUGHT SITUATIONS

Achnatherum	*Elymus*	*Nassella*
Ammophila	*Eragrostis*	*Panicum*
Ampelodesmos	*Festuca*	*Pennisetum*
Aristida	*Helictotrichon*	*Poa*
Austrostipa	*Jarava*	*Sesleria*
Bothriochloa	*Leymus*	*Sporobolus*
Bouteloua	*Muhlenbergia*	*Stipa*
Calamagrostis such as *C. foliosa*		

Grasses for Woodland and Shade

Shade is not the natural setting for most true grasses. Yet shade is found in just about every garden, with dry shade in particular widely regarded as the most difficult of the cultural conditions under which to plant successfully.

True grasses, which mostly have their origins in open sunlit areas, are generally least able to cope with the shady conditions found in gardens, though there are a few notable exceptions such as the wild oat or spangle grass, *Chasmanthium latifolium*. Occurring naturally in shady woodland areas, it translates easily into a wide range of shady garden situations, making it a valuable exception to the general rule. It is also a really first-class garden plant whose wiry upright stems support thin green leaves that are in turn topped by very flat spangle-shaped heads of flower. Wild oat has real character and is a great addition to any shady planting area.

What will actually grow where depends very much on how much light is available. While it is fairly certain that confirmed sun-worshippers such as *Pennisetum* and *Eragrostis* are unlikely to approve of anything but full sun, the light levels encountered in, say, mediterranean areas will allow a greater tolerance from a larger number of grasses than would be possible in colder and less sunny climates. For example in the comparatively warm and dry climate of Arroyo Grande, California, in the garden of Dave and Rainie Fross, sun-loving *Helictotrichon sempervirens* along with other blue-foliaged grasses can be found happily ensconced in still very dry, but also far more shady, conditions than it could possibly tolerate in areas of lower light and heat.

As a general rule shade is very much the province of the grass allies, those plants that are not botanically grasses but have a superficial resemblance in one way or another to the grass family. Generally characterized by comparatively compact evergreen foliage, as well as flowers that are outshone by this foliage, examples include *Carex, Luzula, Ophiopogon* and *Juncus*. The turf lilies (*Ophiopogon*) provide understated elegance wherever they are used, their neat evergreen foliage seemingly impervious to the amount of shade or the dryness of the soil.

Wild oat, *Chasmanthium latifolium* (left), is one of relatively few true grasses that come from woodland conditions. With wide light green leaves and an upright habit, producing masses of distinctive flattened flowers, it is much underused in gardens.

Sun-loving, drought-tolerant blue-foliaged grasses such as *Helictotrichon sempervirens* (below, in back on the left), festuca (below, middle left) and sesleria (below, front right) grow happily under the very dry and comparatively shady conditions found in the mediterranean-climate garden of Dave and Rainie Fross in Arroyo Grande, California.

In fairly dense shade the dwarf mondo grass, *Ophiopogon japnicus* 'Minor', gradually makes reliably close carpets of dark green foliage in effective contrast to the more solid stones, paving blocks and surrounding large-leaved hostas at Chanticleer Gardens in Pennsylvania.

Among the most popular of these grass-like plants is the black mondo grass, *Ophiopogon planiscapus* 'Nigrescens', which seems equally happy in sun or shade. Its foliage is about the closest to pure black you can get in the plant world and it has tiny bluish white flowers and occasional fruits nearly the same colour as the foliage. The best performer for shade is the more infrequently seen green form, *Ophiopogon planiscapus*, which has tighter clumps of foliage that hardly if ever need attention so that it comes as close to being maintenance-free as any plant can. Nearly ten years ago at Knoll, we planted narrow drifts of *O. planiscapus* at what was the edge of a large silver maple's leaf canopy; the plants have grown and flourished in the dry rooty shade, and have yet

to require any maintenance other than occasional raking of fallen leaves from the maple.

Carex, the sedges, are a particularly large and adaptable group. Some can be found growing successfully in most levels of shade, and in very wet to almost-dust-dry soils. Sedges have given rise to many different cultivars, especially variegated-leaved forms which along with the species have become almost indispensable to successful shade planting. Again at Knoll, in the dry shade under large established shrubs, *Carex morrowii* 'Ice Dance' has created a most satisfying cover of creamy-white-striped green leaves that appear entirely indifferent to the dryness and lack of sun. Other first-class selections include the long-established

The gradually spreading, rather than mounding, habit of *Carex morrowii* 'Ice Dance' makes for practical and durable ground cover as part of a public planting in New York.

almost-white *C. oshimensis* 'Evergold' or the slightly finer leaved *C.* 'Silver Sceptre'. In contrast, *Carex divulsa* has a plain green leaf but its neat rounded habit and ability to perform in a wide variety of environments places it firmly in the front rank.

Shade itself can come in many different forms. It ranges from the light, open shade of a fenceline or single-storey building, through more serious levels of shade and rain shadow in the lee of larger buildings and distant woody plants, to the severely limiting dry shade to be found under the canopies and within reach of the questing root systems of established trees.

The comparatively open shade cast by fences, buildings and other non-living objects is often easier to accommodate, as there are no root systems from large established trees or shrubs with which new plants have to contend. What's more, while direct access to the sun may be physically denied, the surrounding area can still be relatively open so that light levels are frequently sufficient to sustain a wide range of plant growth. In such situations, not only will the shade-tolerant grasses and sedges such as *Deschampsia*, *Molinia* and *Carex* do well, but some of the main groups of grasses such as *Miscanthus* and *Panicum* may also find enough sunlight to thrive.

In fact, certain miscanthus may appear to be quite happy in a reasonable amount of shade. *Miscanthus sinensis* 'Abundance', for example, well-named for its enthusiastically produced masses of flower, grows well at Knoll in the shade of larger shrubs, and while not cut off entirely from any direct sunshine it contends successfully with dry soils and other established root systems. Miscanthus chosen for their foliage rather than flower also seem to cope pretty well with noticeable amounts of shade. Elsewhere in the garden *Miscanthus sinensis* var. *condensatus* 'Cosmopolitan', with its wide healthy green-and-white leaves, has been growing in the shade of trees and bamboo for some years and while perhaps not as large or exhuberant as when grown in easier conditions appears quite tolerant of these challenges. *Miscanthus sinensis* 'Dixieland', *M. s.* 'Variegatus' and even the striking *M. s.* var. *condensatus* 'Cabaret' seem to cope remarkably well in various degrees of shade.

Heavy shade cast by established trees and shrubs is the most difficult in which to plant successfully, whether with grasses or any other group of plants. This is because the lack of light is combined with extreme dryness at the root, usually at a time when moisture is needed during the active growing period.

Under deciduous trees and shrubs there can often be adequate moisture in the spring period, after the winter rains occur and before the trees leaf out. Spring-flowering bulbs take advantage of this period to flower and then close down as the tree wakes up and the soil starts to dry out. Several grasses have copied this strategy, including the wood melics (*Melica*) and the wood millets (*Milium*), which are at their best

This restful waterside planting of *Carex oshimensis* 'Evergold' at the RHS Garden Wisley in England makes full use of the cultivar's mounding habit. The surrounding woody plants will gradually create more shade. Black mondo grass, *Ophiopogon planiscapus* 'Nigrescens', and tan-orange *Carex testacea* complete the ground pattern.

Most miscanthus flower best when sunlight levels are sufficient to stimulate effective blooming, but foliage forms, which are not grown primarily for their flowers, can tolerate more shade. *Miscanthus sinensis* 'Abundance' produces masses of flowers but appears tolerant of this semi-shady position at Knoll Gardens.

before the dry summer period when they close down until the return of wetter winter conditions. Among the most useful spring-flowerers is the snowy woodrush, *Luzula nivea*, whose tight mounds of green leaves, covered in soft white hairs, are topped by the most subtly beautiful spikes of white or off-white flowers, at their best before soils become too dry. Amazingly adaptable, this woodrush will grow in most types of shade from almost-boggy to fairly dry.

Where tree roots have not entirely taken over the soil, or under younger, less established trees or shrubs, the hakone grasses, *Hakonechloa macra* and its cultivars, can make wonderful longlasting mounds of delicate-looking foliage—a constant delight. Initially somewhat slow-growing, they are very long lived and durable once

established. At Knoll one of the most satisfying of all combinations has resulted from planting *Hakonechloa macra* 'Aureola' ('Alboaurea') in a 3–4-metre (9–12-ft.) circle around the base of a paperbark mulberry. While not in the deepest of shade, the sandy soil and roots of the mulberry ensure frequent dryness during the summer months, which the hakone grass simply shrugs off. The combination of the grass' and bark's textural qualities with the tree's leaves is as immensely satisfying as it is undemanding to maintain.

For conditions ranging from full sun to the driest of shade, the pheasant grass, *Anemanthele lessoniana* (formerly *Stipa arundinacea*), is perhaps the most adaptable and successful of grasses—being not only very tough but also very beautiful and quick growing. Even close to

Luzula nivea, or snowy woodrush, is a rosette-forming plant producing masses of white flowers early in the season. Happiest where soil is not too dry, the common name refers to the silvery hair that can be seen on younger leaves.

Hakone grasses do well in or a reasonable amount of shade (right). At the base of a paperback mulberry, *Hakonechloa macra* 'Aureola' makes graceful, weed-proof and longlasting cover in dry, light shade at Knoll Gardens. Photograph courtesy of Dianna Jazwinski.

Pheasant grass may be the most adaptable grass for all levels of shade (except in combination with wet soils). *Anemanthele lessoniana* (far right) is fast growing, with wider-than-high mounds of of evergreen leaves that continuously change from reds and oranges to greens and yellows. In the Fross garden in California, these well-spaced plants cope admirably with very dry, shady conditions.

large evergreens such as conifers, which offer perhaps the harshest and most unrelenting of dry shade, the pheasant grass is among the likeliest of candidates to survive and prosper.

For rather wetter conditions in shade, the purple moor grass and tufted hair grass, *Molinia* and *Deschampsia* respectively, both occur naturally in wetter soils, and even at the water's edge, in open conditions or where shade is not too dense. Tolerant of even more shade along with wetter soils are a large number of sedges, such as the architectural *Carex muskingumensis*, and woodrushes which thrive in the seasonal variations of flood and drought that these particular areas frequently face. By and large the woodrushes are not the most attention-grabbing of plants, but their ability to tolerate damp, wet conditions in shade makes them most useful for covering areas that other plants might find testing. *Luzula sylvatica*, for example, creates rosettes of green leaves that are truthfully not very exciting, and the variegated form *L. s.* 'Marginata' is scarcely better, but their ability to cover ground in tough conditions is almost unmatched. The golden form *L. s.* 'Aurea' is perhaps the exception; in spring, its bright golden yellow foliage can light up the darkest of corners. (This form should not be sited in full sun as it is inclined to scorch if too hot.)

TOP CHOICES FOR WOODLAND AND SHADE

Anemanthele lessoniana
Calamagrostis such as *C. brachytricha*
Carex, most species and cultivars
Chasmanthium latifolium
Deschampsia cespitosa
Hakonechloa macra and its forms
Hystrix patula
Luzula, most species and forms
Melica, most species and forms
Milium effusum and its forms
Miscanthus, some, especially variegated forms
Molinia caerulea
Ophiopogon, several including *O. planiscapus*
Sesleria, most species especially in higher-sunlight areas

Grasses for Wet and Waterside Positions

Most true grasses do not appreciate wet, boggy, watery conditions.

The very demanding nature of some of the more watery environments has given rise to a specialized group of plants whose specific qualities have not always been appreciated by gardeners. In nature the area where the land meets the water, also known as the transition zone, is in many ways a unique habitat. A brief look at any estuary or river mouth will show a mix of habitat from sandy beaches to boggy soils, along with marshland and plants that have adapted to cope with these conditions as well as a whole ecosystem of associated wildlife that has evolved to thrive there. Often in a state of permanent flux with the regular and sometimes rapid changing of water levels in times of flood or drought, the plants that have adapted to these marginal areas are mostly grass allies such as sedges, rushes and reeds.

Comparatively few true grasses have adapted to really wet environments, though the so-called common reed, *Phragmites australis*, is one very notable exception, covering vast areas of land and water's edge with equal facility. Like the common reed, all such truly adapted grasses, and some grass-like plants such as *Glyceria*, *Juncus* and *Schoenoplectus*, have a running rootstock that can move swiftly in order to survive in the constantly changing conditions of their natural homes. However this strategy can make them less than welcome in the more controlled conditions of the average garden unless they are used in very wet conditions such as stream sides, boggy areas or lakes and ponds.

For practical purposes, grasses that can tolerate wet soils, which are usually around or in proximity to water, could be placed in one of two broad categories: those that prefer to paddle and those that don't mind swimming. Paddlers are those grasses that are able to thrive with a fair amount of moisture in the ground for extended periods. While they will tolerate heavy clays that are often waterlogged, on the whole they prefer solid ground. Swimmers, on the other hand, will be happy in permanently wet to open water conditions. By definition most swimmers also make happy, if enthusiastic, paddlers.

Most sedges such as *Carex muskingumensis*, cotton grasses such as

Vast areas of river mouth, wetlands, lakes, open water and estuary play host to a relatively small number of species, such as reeds and rushes, which thrive in wet, stagnant to fast-flowing conditions that are permanently in limbo, somewhere between solid ground and open water.

Eriophorum angustifolium, woodrushes such as *Luzula sylvatica*, and the purple moor grass, *Molinia caerulea*, are paddlers. They are at home in a range of soil conditions from sometimes-dry to damp to wet to water-logged, but still grow primarily in soil rather than water.

Given the wide range of tolerance and adaptability that many grasses display, it is also quite possible to find specimens of the main groups of true grasses such as *Miscanthus* and *Panicum* growing in very wet soils, including heavy clay, even right up to the edge of open water. However, a grass is usually most tolerant in its native area and may consequently be less forgiving when used as an exotic in a garden or designed space. For example, the prairie switch grass, *Panicum virgatum*, is tolerant of wet conditions, and can even be found growing with its feet in water in

Common cotton grass, *Eriophorum angustifolium*, thrives in the open yet boggy conditions of a nature reserve a short distance across open water from the busy urban centre of Poole, Dorset, England.

the New Jersey Pine Barrens where it is locally native, but is unlikely to be as tolerant in the maritime conditions of the U.K.

In the inspirational gardens of Beth Chatto at Elmstead Market in England, the waterside plantings include not only *Carex elata* 'Aurea' and *Molinia caerulea* subsp. *caerulea* 'Variegata', which are native and happy alongside or even *in* the water, but also *Miscanthus sinensis* 'Zebrinus'. Planted just a little further away from the water's edge, the miscanthus will no doubt be able to draw on the relatively high water table and also cope perhaps with an occasional flooding, but nonetheless remains for the most part on comparatively solid ground.

The swimmers include reeds and rushes such as *Juncus*, *Phragmites*, *Typha* and *Schoenoplectus* whose strong, mobile root systems are equally

Panicum virgatum, the prairie switch grass, tolerates wide-ranging conditions from drought to water's edge where its stout root system can help to prevent erosion, as seen on the lake edge at Chicago Botanic Garden.

at home in solid ground but have evolved to deal successfully with the shifting ground, or lack of it, in a watery environment. Their ability to travel over such a variety of conditions gives many coastal and lakeside areas their characteristic look and feel and is the prime reason for their successful and increasing use in stabilization and erosion control projects. While some such as *Phragmites*, even in its comparatively restrained variegated form *P. australis* subsp. *australis* 'Variegatus', may not be suitable for the smallest garden areas, several make the perfect accent in ponds and smaller water features, including those with comparatively restrained ornamental forms such as *Schoenoplectus lacustris* subsp. *tabernaemontani* 'Albescens' with its unique light green and cream longitudinal stripes on brittle rounded stems. For a more bulky

DESIGNING WITH GRASSES

This masterful planting in Beth Chatto's renowned gardens in Essex, England uses *Miscanthus sinensis* 'Zebrinus' (centre left), *Carex elata* 'Aurea' (centre) and *Molinia caerulea* subsp. *caerulea* 'Variegata' (far right) in successful association with larger-leaved plants such as the giant rhubarb, *Gunnera tinctoria*, which are happy in the usually damp soils at the water's edge.

but still controllable plant, the attractively variegated *Spartina pectinata* 'Aureomarginata' is a good choice to associate with other moisture-loving perennials such as *Eupatorium*, *Lythrum* and *Filipendula*.

Several moisture-lovers such as *Juncus*, *Luzula* and various species and cultivars of *Carex* are recommended for being able to cope with rather dry and shady conditions, which initially appears as something of a contradiction considering their native habitats. But most wet soils, whether by open water, pure heavy soils or open boggy moorland, can become drier (and sometimes even dry out completely) as part of an annual cycle, and as a result many damp-loving plants have had to adapt to deal with such periods of relative drought. Sedges in particular are very adept at this; many species such as *Carex divulsa*, *C. remota*, *C.*

Used historically for matting and thatching, the common club rush, *Schoenoplectus lacustris* subsp. *tabernaemontani*, makes dense colonies in rivers and open water (above, centre), providing cover and forage for wildlife as well as an ornamental feature for the local human population in Wimborne, Dorset, England.

Carex secta, a graceful sedge from New Zealand, grows happily in the boggy waterlogged soil introduced into a man-made pond at Knoll Gardens (right).

praegracilis, *C. elata* and *C. obnupta* can tolerate relatively dry soils provided they receive the occasional long drink from rainfall or irrigation.

Where no natural water exists, introducing it into the designed space can result in a hard and frequently unsympathetic margin between the water and the rest of the garden. Swimming pools and formal ponds are common culprits, so often appearing as afterthoughts that are almost completely disconnected from the rest of the garden design.

Planting grasses close to such features, at least on one side, helps to soften the demarcation between water and ground, linking the water feature with the rest of the garden. Where the soil conditions are not affected by the water's proximity, choose any grasses that can cope with the prevailing soil conditions, which may be quite ordinary to dry. Sun-loving grasses such as the fountain grasses or *Pennisetum* species, for example, can be superb at gracing the surrounding areas of a garden pool, where their rounded outline and bottlebrush-like flowers contrast with, and are often mirrored in, the flatness of the water's surface. *Miscanthus sinensis* 'Morning Light' is another excellent choice, with a clear vase-like outline that stands out particularly effectively against a background of open water.

One simple but highly effective water feature for gardens with no natural water is a 'low-tech' sloping-sided pond. With no clear division between the water and the surrounding soil, this type of pool allows for the development of a transition zone in which many of the more gardenworthy moisture-lovers such as star sedge, *Rhynchospora*, and cotton grass, *Eriophorum*, can be grown. Sited in a lower part of the garden, lined if desired, not necessarily too deep and requiring no special attention in the form of filtering or cleaning, such ponds always seem to attract wildlife. They are easy to maintain and constantly interesting.

Where a steep-sided, more formal pond is already in existence, it can be quite easily converted to make a whole new planting habitat in an otherwise dry garden. For example, at Knoll we had a formal rectangular pond only about 45 cm (18 in.) deep, with brick sides and a base of butyl liner. Hard paving surrounded more than half of its perimeter, the rest being border, and there was no filtration. With water that turned green in warm weather, the feature left much to be desired—in fact, it seemed rather pointless.

But as the garden consisted almost entirely of dry sand with very little moisture, this outdated water feature offered a perfect opportunity to create a self-sustaining watery habitat that was otherwise absent from the garden. Sandy soil, not too rich in nutrients, was simply barrowed directly into the pond in sufficient quantities to make small islands of soil that appeared just above the usual level of the water after settling, leaving about half of the pond as open water.

TOP CHOICES FOR WET AND WATERSIDE POSITIONS

Paddlers

Carex, most species and forms

Cyperus, most species

Eriophorum, most species

Juncus, some species such as *J. inflexus* and *J. effusus* and forms

Luzula, most species

Miscanthus, some species such as *M.* ×*giganteus*, and *M. sinensis* in warmer climates

Molinia caerulea and its forms

Phalaris arundinacea and its forms

Rhynchospora, most species

Swimmers

Arundo donax and its forms

Carex, some such as *C. elata* 'Aurea'

Cyperus, most species

Glyceria species and forms

Juncus, some species such as *J. militaris*; others prefer to paddle

Phragmites australis and its forms

Schoenoplectus, most species

Spartina pectinata and its forms

Moisture-lovers that now excel in the boggy soils include the lesser bulrush, *Typha angustifolia*, while *Molinia caerulea* subsp. *arundinacea* and even *Arundo donax* 'Macrophylla' rub shoulders with *Eupatorium lindleyanum* and *Eupatorium maculatum* Atropurpureum Group. *Juncus effusus* has seeded in the shady corners next to the distinctive foliage of *Carex muskingumensis*, and the delicate and longlasting star sedge, *Rhynchospora latifolia*, displays its incredible white flowers close to the paving. *Carex elata* 'Aurea', always distinctive in ordinary soils with its golden yellow leaves topped with yellow and black flowers in late spring, is even more robust and obviously very happy. *Carex secta*, a subtly beautiful evergreen sedge from New Zealand, has meanwhile developed into a huge ball-shaped specimen that simply demands admiration the moment it is seen. Apart from some annual tidying, this area has required virtually no attention—at least, not from the gardener; it gets much attention from myriad forms of life including frogs, toads, dragon flies and damsel flies, grass snakes and slow worms.

Grasses for Pots and Containers

Easy to grow on the whole, grasses are no less obliging when grown in containers provided their basic needs such as water, light and adequate root run are met. Indeed, for many gardeners some of the slower-to-establish grasses perform better in pots than in open ground, at least in their early years. One example is the Japanese blood grass, *Imperata cylindrica* 'Rubra', which can be very slow to establish in the open ground; in its native Japan it has been grown for many decades in shallow dishes as a companion to bonsai.

In many respects, container-grown grasses demand the same considerations as other container-grown plants. Drought-loving grasses will (unsurprisingly) tolerate less water than moisture-lovers, and those slower growers like the hakone grass, *Hakonechloa macra* and its forms, will survive happily for longer without being re-potted. However, attention to irrigation, pot size and growing medium is necessary for successful container growing.

Some grasses that are grown primarily for their foliage are especially effective in taller containers, as this allows the foliage to gradually trail downwards and develop a more pendulous habit than the grasses would manage when planted in the ground. For example, the purple-tinged foliage of *Eragrostis curvula* 'Totnes Burgundy' deepens in colour as the season progresses and if grown in a sufficiently tall container it gradually develops a distinct weeping habit that is quite special. The flowers of this wonderful form, especially when grown in pots, can distract from the foliage and are often best removed for maximum impact.

Certain evergreen sedges can also develop this habit. For instance, the tan-coloured leaves of *Carex testacea* seem to extend much further than their normal length when given the opportunity. And while in open ground the flowers of *C. testacea* and of other species such as *C. dipsacea* are usually insignificant, passing virtually unnoticed, in a tall container they appear to adopt the same extended weeping habit as the leaves; at Knoll we have seen them extend to well over 1 metre (3 ft.) long, making a quite spectacular display.

A collection of plants in containers, whether entirely grasses or a mix of plants in differing shapes and sizes, can make for a very satisfying display in a relatively limited space over a long period of time. Individual containers can be rearranged or replaced, allowing for a constantly changing matrix of flower and form to delight and refresh the senses.

Grasses which are borderline, or distinctly non-hardy for the area where they are being grown, can be more easily protected from frost when grown in containers that can be moved at short notice so that plants are kept warm and/or dry as required during the colder months. For example, *Pennisetum ×advena* 'Rubrum' and *Cyperus papyrus* are two architectural but non-hardy grasses that can be grown successfully in cooler climates using containers.

On hard surfaces like terraces close to the house, or where soil or space is lacking such as on roof gardens or balconies, the thoughtful use of containers is a successful way of providing a home for plants. And with a little ingenuity, as much interest can be gained from the containers as from the plants themselves. Whether of horticultural origin or not, any suitable receptacle can be pressed into service as long as it will hold the growing medium (compost) and allows water to drain. However, it is genuinely true that the more capacious the container, the longer and better the plant will grow.

Grasses need not always be planted in the pots to make an effective association with containers (above). The clever placing of a single empty pot at Chanticleer in Pennsylvania uses the relatively solid shape of the container in effective contrast to the effervescent outline of nearby groups of *Panicum virgatum*.

The strong linear outline of most grasses contrasts effectively with more solid objects, especially when made of natural materials such as terracotta and wood (left). The association is no less effective during the quieter winter period.

Containers made of wood, stone or other natural material usually make the most satisfying associations with plants, and this is particularly so with the strong linear outline of grasses. The simpler geometric outlines of circles and squares combined with finishes that develop an ever-changing patina with increasing age, such as rusty metal, may provide the greatest satisfaction in terms of contrast between plant and container.

A tall, elegant container (right) allows *Carex testacea* to display bronzed evergreen foliage that appears to gradually creep ever downwards—a trait that would be lost were it planted at ground level.

Most grasses with fibrous root systems are happy in containers, provided they are watered when dry and re-potted when necessary. Containers also allow you to grow plants that would be considered at risk if grown in the open ground in certain areas, such as *Jarava ichu* which forms part of the entrance container display at Knoll Gardens (below).

Magnificent stone urns at the end of the famous canal at the RHS Garden Wisley in Surrey, England provide a perfect traditional setting for the distinctive outline of *Miscanthus sinensis* 'Morning Light'.

TOP CHOICES FOR POTS AND CONTAINERS

Virtually all grasses work well in pots, but several stand out as being especially suitable:

Anemanthele lessoniana
Carex, especially foliage forms such as *C. testacea* and
  C. dipsacea
Cyperus papyrus
Eragrostis curvula 'Totnes Burgundy'
Festucas such as *F. glauca* 'Siskiyou Blue'
Hakonechloa, all forms
Imperata cylindrica 'Rubra'
Jarava ichu (formerly *Stipa ichu*)
Miscanthus, compact forms such as *M. sinensis* 'Little Kitten'
  or *M.s.* 'Abundance'
Pennisetum, all forms but especially *P.* ×*advena* 'Rubrum'

SEVEN

Grasses for a Greener World

MORE AND MORE, garden plants are being used not just for aesthetic reasons but also for ecologically friendly purposes, encompassed by the relatively new term 'functional horticulture'. Several applications of functional horticulture, including lawn replacement, erosion control, habitat restoration, green roofs and rain gardens, are set to increase rapidly in importance and popularity as a greater number of gardeners wake up to their value. And increasingly, using native plants in the garden is an appealing option.

While a detailed account of such processes is rather beyond the scope of this book, given the amazing versatility and adaptability that grasses exhibit it will be no surprise to see them figure highly in these practical and often environmentally based horticultural applications—many of which are suitable for gardens of all sizes.

In the New Jersey Pine Barrens this carpet of sedge, *Carex pensylvanica*, is naturally occurring and requires absolutely no maintenance.

Don't Mow It—Grow It: the Alternative Lawn

Found across many cultures and under most climatic conditions, lawns are among the most enduringly popular of garden features. Traditional, high-quality lawns can be very impressive; for instance, when surrounding historic buildings they create a clear feeling of open space and provide easy access for foot traffic. (Ironically, though, many of the best lawns prohibit foot traffic in order to preserve their pristine appearance and display them as horticultural showpieces.) Yet such superb lawns are mostly very demanding in terms of time and resources needed to maintain them.

Alternatives to regularly cut grass swards are valuable primarily when environmental or financial costs of maintaining the traditional lawn are unacceptably high, or where cultural or environmental factors such as deep shade or arid, dry conditions prohibit the successful establishment of a more traditional green sward.

Another powerful argument for alternative lawns comes from a purely aesthetic standpoint: sometimes there is little value in maintaining an unsatisfactory or average traditional lawn when a looser less formal finish, often termed 'the meadow look', makes for a more stimulating feature with much less effort on the part of the gardener. Many unsatisfactory lawns probably linger today simply because their owners are unaware of the alternative possibilities.

Indeed, I have long found that many traditional lawns serve little purpose and offer little value considering the level of attention and resources they demand. Think of the typical house, with a small lawn at the front of the property, which must be kept looking tidy but otherwise performs no useful or essential function except perhaps allowing access to the building or other garden areas. When the whole garden area is quite small, and consists of a small lawn, a narrow flowerbed or two and perhaps a hedge or foundation planting, the lawn takes up valuable space that could otherwise be devoted to more interesting plantings.

In mild and often wet conditions such as those found throughout much of the U.K., the average lawn may only need cutting during the

summer months, and possibly a few waterings if not left to go dormant in dry summers (which would also lessen the need for regular mowing, if also lessening the aesthetic value). While still performing no real function, such a lawn may be less burdensome than one in such warm and dry conditions as found in, say, southern California, which would require far more mowing and especially irrigation in an area that is already short of such precious resources.

While often serving little use from either a design or a practical viewpoint, en masse these traditional lawns consume a vast amount of resources that would be better conserved for use elsewhere. Simply

In Tenerife this lawn prohibits foot traffic and needs regular watering and attention to maintain its impeccable condition, unlike the carpet of sedge on pages 124–125.

A variety of low-growing grasses can recreate the effect of traditional open lawn at a fraction of its maintenence cost. The hakone grass, *Hakonechloa macra*, used here at the front of the new glasshouse at the RHS Garden Wisley, England, contrasts effectively with trimmed beech cylinders.

removing the lawn altogether (perhaps along with all of the other too-small garden features), and replacing it with a single carpet-like planting of grasses as a 'meadow' through which other plants such as bulbs summer flowers, and shrubs can grow, not only reduces the workload but makes a far more successful garden feature. Pathways can dissect the 'carpet' wherever necessary for access or simply for passing through.

Suitable grasses for such alternative lawns are usually compact and evergreen, with spreading rootstocks that can effectively renew themselves to maintain a good, even cover much as a traditional lawn grass might do. Any grass or grass-like plant with this attribute is therefore a candidate, but in practice much depends on the amount of wear or foot traffic it is likely to receive; a more limited number of plants will accept regular trampling.

An excellent example is in fact not a true grass but the western meadow sedge, *Carex praegracilis*. Native to a large part of the western United States in a range of situations from coastal sand dunes to inland meadows, this sedge is being used successfully in many areas across the U.S. Like other forms of *Carex*, this spreading sedge makes dense cover, remaining green with enough water and eventually going summer-dormant in prolonged drought. At the University of California's Leaning Pine Arboretum in San Luis Obispo, for instance, this meadow sedge is used as a regularly mowed lawn of considerable size— and its amazing adaptability has seen its use in many private gardens, where it can be cut on a regular basis, to the point where it becomes virtually indistinguishable from a more traditional sward. However, it is arguably at it most eloquent when forming a shaggy evergreen cover that is cut as rarely as once or twice each year.

Eschewing a more traditional layout, Dave and Rainie Fross have planted a private garden in Arroyo Grande, California, with a system of informal pathways threading their way unhurriedly though grassy plantings. The result is a superlative essay in achieving the natural meadow effect, where plantings of *Carex praegracili*s are allowed to grow unchecked by the lawn mower, requiring perhaps a once-a-year trim, to produce a lush sward that is highly pleasing and entirely appropriate to its place and function.

The mondo grasses are often used as replacement covering, especially in shade where traditional grass swards will not survive. *Ophiopogon planiscapus* will make superb cover even in dry shade under trees, and needs virtually no maintenance, but will tolerate much less foot traffic than will the western meadow sedge. *Ophiopogon japonicus* 'Minor' has the smallest of leaves that make a complete cover only a few centimetres high, but again it is only for areas that are not regularly trodden.

Laying an alternative lawn is relatively easy. In many respects it is like planting any border or flower bed, but with a few special considerations:

Western meadow sedge, *Carex praegracilis* (above), can cover large areas and has a well-established reputation as a successful lawn substitute. Native to much of the western U.S. under a variety of conditions from coastal sand dune to inland meadows, it has a spreading rootstock that allows it to withstand regular cutting and a substantial amount of foot traffic. In the private Los Angeles garden on the right, the lawn is composed entirely of *Carex praegracilis*, irrigated as necessary with grey water from inside the house.

Carex praegracilis (above, towards the back) is used as part of the meadow matrix of grasses and sedges to lend a softer, more relaxed feel to the private garden of Dave and Rainie Fross.

- Remove any existing turf and loosen ground if compacted, then rake and prepare to a reasonably level finish.
- Avoid too fussy an outline; circles and gently curving edges are more satisfying and natural looking. Better still, to create a great sense of space, treat grasses as you would a wall-to-wall carpet indoors; plant right up to other features or boundaries, avoiding a clear edge.
- If possible, use smaller plants at high density, rather than a smaller number of larger plants, to make their establishment noticeably quicker.
- For a more traditional-lawn-like finish, especially one that is to be trimmed regularly, take care to plant at the same spacing throughout to provide the most even cover in the shortest time.
- After planting, use a surface mulch such as bark or gravel to allow the area to be used more quickly.

- Pathways, if needed, can be made from the same material as the surface mulch and allowed to meander through or around the new planting.
- Bear in mind that many lawn alternatives will need a little trimming. Some like *Carex* and *Deschampsia* will need a once-a-year cut using a trimmer for the shaggy meadow look, though they will accept more regular cuts with a lawn mower set relatively high. Others such as *Ophiopogon planiscapus* will virtually never need trimming.

TOP CHOICES FOR LAWN ALTERNATIVES

Briza media, for light use

Buchloe, most species

Carex, many species, especially those with spreading rootstock such as *C. praegracilis*, and *Carex flacca* for lighter use

Deschampsia, especially *D. cespitosa* and seed strains bred specifically for lawn use

Festuca rubra and its forms

Koeleria, several including *K. macrantha*

Ophiopogon, several species and forms, especially *O. planiscapus* although it does not tolerate much foot traffic

Grasses for Erosion Control

As our homes and gardens extend outwards, they are in ever-closer proximity to beaches and their shifting sands. Consequently, plants once regarded as 'weedy' beach grasses of no real value are now seen as valuable tools that can solve a problem without recourse to often unsuccessful and always expensive engineered solutions of block and concrete. For instance, *Panicum amarum*, a coast-adapted species from the Eastern Seaboard of the United States, is both a beautiful and a practical choice for stabilization in these areas.

While a vigorous, self-renewing, dense, spreading root system may not characterize the ideal garden plant, it is essential if that plant is to deal effectively with unstable sand or soil. For example, on the beaches around Poole in Dorset, England, as in many other places lyme grass, *Leymus arenarius*, and other specially adapted beach grasses such as marram, *Ammophila arenaria*, help to stabilize and control the movement of the sand dunes, in the process creating a more stable environment for themselves and other wildlife.

Not all of us can live on a beach, but many gardens have soil banks in varying degrees of steepness which in many respects are similar to the shifting sands; soil banks are known for their ability to slip, especially in wet weather. Such problems are often controlled by engineered solutions such as retaining walls, which are never cheap, frequently ugly and difficult to disguise. In many situations, even steep banks can be controlled and stabilized by the use of dense-rooting, mat-forming plants such as *Carex praegracilis*, *Phragmites australis* or *Leymus arenarius*, which cover the surface and whose robust root systems will bind the soil together.

With banks that are less steep, a much wider range of grasses—which do not necessarily need such a vigorous spreading root system—can be used successfully. Often in such situations erosion is principally a wind-related problem, especially prevalent with dry soils in that the wind will gradually carry off the top layers of soil over an extended period. Establishing any kind of cover will stop or slow this process and any of the grasses above along with *Aristida*, *Nassella*, *Melica* and *Stipa* can be used.

Planting a bank is not much different from any other garden planting. For best results, consider the following:

• The steeper the bank, the more a vigorous root system is needed.
• Always use beach grasses for shifting sand, as they are adapted for such extreme conditions.

A steep bank between a private garden and a public highway in Monterey, California (above) is prevented from slipping or eroding by the use of a native sedge, *Carex praegracilis*, which in its summer-dormant state mirrors the surrounding hillsides almost perfectly.

Lyme grass, *Leymus arenarius*, helps to stabilize and conserve the sandy dunes on a beach in Dorset, England (right).

BEACH ZONING
CONSERVATION AREA

THIS FENCED AREA OF THE BEACH IS A
LOCAL CONSERVATION AREA

BEACH USERS ARE REQUESTED
NOT TO ENTER THIS AREA

Information

Poole
IT'S A BEAUTIFUL PLACE

- Quick establishment is always the goal, so plant at greater densities, perhaps using twice the usual recommended number of plants per square metre.
- A greater number of smaller plants will often establish and make a complete cover more easily than fewer larger plants.
- On steeper banks, or where loose soil is inclined to move around, use a covering mulch of matting that can be pegged down onto the soil. Netting can also be used if appropriate.

Grasses for Habitat Restoration

The term 'habitat restoration' usually describes the returning of an area to the vegetative population that occupied it at some point in the recent past. Often this involves removing existing aggressive exotic species and replacing them with native plants that were themselves gradually displaced by the colonizing exotics. It is often carried out in areas where there has been direct, frequently short-term, human interference such as the laying of pipelines, civil engineering work or even the building of new homes; after these projects end, it is desirable to return the area to something resembling its original natural state. Sometimes 'site-specific' projects are carried out; when an area is due to be disrupted, plants (usually native) are collected, propagated and then later returned to a site once work has been completed.

On the coastal fringe of Monterey, California, in the narrow strips between a golf links and the ocean, garden designer Fred Ballerini and his team have piloted a successful scheme to turn this overlooked area back into its valuable habitat. The area had become covered with aggressive exotics such as the ever-popular ice plant which, while perhaps aesthetically pleasing to the casual eye, had effectively managed to stifle everything else in its path. As a first step, the ice plant covering much of the area's forty acres was mechanically bulldozed and buried, with any regrowth being spot-sprayed and left as a mulch. As a result many native plants, including the saltgrass, *Distichlis spicata*, started an almost immediate and determined comeback. New plants germinated from the seed bank that was dormant but still viable in the underlying soil, and were quick to take advantage of the opportunity to recover

Stabilized sand dunes adjoining a coastal golf links in Monterey, California had become overgrown with exotics, such as the ice plant, to the detriment of native plants and grasses—until a rigorously planned programme of restoration brought about the successful return of many native grasses, sedges and rushes (above). The native salt grass, *Distichlis spicata*, seen on the right emerging from the dead remains of ice plants, needed very little encouragement to return from the seed bank remaining in the sand.

lost ground. Several years on, the area now has a healthy mixed population of natives including grasses, sedges and rushes that are self sustaining and make a far greater contribution to the area's biodiversity.

Historically, habitat restoration has been seen as the province of nature reserves and natural parks, rather than gardens and designed spaces. But as more and more homes infringe on natural areas, and as we gain greater understanding of the importance of preserving the natural landscape and maintaining biodiversity, an increased blurring of the lines between natural and designed areas will see the value and relevance of restoration projects increase many times over in the coming years.

In northern California's Marin County, this garden designed by Bernard Trainor surrounds a new hilltop home and uses Californian poppy, Sonoma sage, and native grasses such as *Nassella pulchra* and *Muhlenbergia rigens* as part of a restrained and sophisticated palette—merging the newly designed elements with the natural landscape, and restoring some of what was lost during the building process.
Photograph courtesy of Jason Liske.

Grasses for Green Roofs

In use for almost as long as humans have been building houses, green roofs—where living plant material is used as a roof covering for homes and buildings—are not exactly new. As urban, industrial areas take up ever more space, green roofs have seen increased popularity for their eco-friendly ability to modify and control major environmental issues such as the general loss of biodiversity, the creation of heat island effects and the increased risk from stormwater flooding.

With the construction of any building, from a basic garden shed to a multi-storey parking lot, the ground it occupies becomes unable to support any biodiversity. Installing a green roof helps to replace at least part of that loss, and making up for this building's 'footprint' can be furthered through the appropriate use of locally native plants. Apart from their aesthetic appeal, such roofs' demonstrable benefits include a reduction of energy consumption, and the control of stormwater runoff due to the sponge-like nature of an established green roof, which gradually releases water over a much longer period than a traditional roof would.

Green roofs are frequently described as either 'extensive' or 'intensive'. Extensive roofs tend to cover larger areas, but with a shallow depth of substrate that restricts the choice of plant. Intensive roofs tend to be smaller in area but have a greater depth of substrate that allows a wider choice of plants, they are slightly reminiscent of more traditional roof gardens.

On a domestic scale, with a little knowledge and preparation, green roofs can be fitted to small outbuildings, garden sheds and even kennels relatively easily. As a green roof can add considerable weight to the loading of a roof structure, it is advisable to consult building professionals or specialist green roof firms before commencing any project.

A variety of plants including grasses and sedges make excellent green roof subjects, though as conditions can be difficult—extreme dryness, a shallow root run and searing temperatures are an issue in many situations—toughness is perhaps the plants' prime requirement. Similar in some respects to lawn alternatives, a spreading, self-renewing, compact

habit is a distinct advantage as this helps to create a dense self-sustaining mat that binds the roof together.

As with banks and lawn replacement schemes, a great number of smaller plants makes a more satisfactory cover than a lesser number of larger plants. Planting density depends partly on the actual size of the plants, so that while larger plants may be used at (for instance) fifteen per square metre, smaller plug-sized plants might be used at twice that number.

Roof gardens such as this one in downtown San Francisco are gaining popularity as their positive effects on human welfare and their value for energy conservation begin to be fully realized. *Festuca* and *Carex* combine in an attractive mosaic designed by Dave Fross.

TOP CHOICES FOR GREEN ROOFS

Bouteloua	*Deschampsia*	*Sesleria*
Briza	*Festuca*	*Sporobolus*
Carex		

Grasses for Rain Gardens

Green roofs are an important part of the ethos of rain gardens, which themselves offer a complete alternative approach to using water in our gardens and urban spaces. Rain gardens challenge the more traditional view of water, so often regarded as either an individual 'feature' effectively divorced from the rest of the landscape or, especially in the case of urban stormwater, simply an irritation to be drained or culverted away at the earliest opportunity.

Low-impact design lies at the heart of the rain garden, where water is regarded as having a natural cycle that is both accommodated and used to benefit biodiversity. Natural water is often controlled through a series of features and plantings (often termed 'bioretention'), much as a green roof might do but at the ground level and over a much wider area.

With their sponge-like ability to soak up moisture, to release water into the atmosphere, to filter and to cleanse, plants are an integral part of the bioretention process. Using plants at ground level (as opposed to on rooftops), eco-minded gardeners looking to conserve water can choose from a wider range of plants—including a palette of grasses that are both functional and beautiful.

TOP CHOICES FOR RAIN GARDENS

Acorus	*Juncus*	*Phragmites*
Calamagrostis	*Luzula*	*Schoenoplectus*
Carex	*Molinia*	*Typha*
Eriophorum	*Panicum*	

Going Native

The day of the native ornamental is drawing near.
    —Douglas Tallamy, *Bringing Nature Home*

Gardening literature, and even culture, is littered with references to native plants as weeds, regardless of whether they are grasses or any

This rain garden at the Tabor School in the United States was designed to catch and absorb water runoff from buildings and other structures, avoiding the need for expensive stormwater runoff systems and allowing the water to infiltrate the soil rather than being removed from the area where it is most needed. Photograph courtesy of Edmund C. Snodgrass.

other plants. And it is possible to understand this long-established link between weeds and natives; historically, gardens were intentionally artificial creations, filled with exotic introductions. Imposed on the natural landscape, these exotics necessarily displaced the native species which were regarded simply as unwanted plants. As one of the most common wild plants, grasses in particular have historically been removed in favour of non-natives.

These days, however, as we wake up to the true value of our natural systems and our collective impact on them, the definition of a weed is coming full circle to include many of those introduced exotic species, which often have aggressive tendencies to colonize, displace or disrupt the original communities of plants. An old saying has it that 'a weed is a plant in the wrong place', and for all its simplicity this has to remain among the most valid and accurate of gardening observations.

The iconic grasslands so often depicted in popular images of California are in fact largely composed of exotic European species, introduced in attempts to improve grazing. While these exotics supplant native grasses in most areas, highly serpentine soils present a barrier that allows the better-adapted native grasses to survive and even prosper.

WHAT IS A NATIVE?   At first glance, and quite straightforwardly, a native plant could be regarded as coming from a distinct geographical area such as Europe or, more specifically, Germany. On the other hand, 'exotic' or 'alien' would describe a plant that did not naturally occur in that area but that had been introduced there (usually through human agency). A further category; that of a 'naturalized' species, describes an exotic that has been in its new home for sufficient time to be regarded, at least by some, as almost native.

However, given the vast areas, differing climates and local conditions that such broad terms encompass, these words can often be effectively meaningless and even counterproductive when it comes to the practice of garden-making and the process of choosing plants. For example a grass may be said to be a European native, but this does not necessarily mean it is a U.K. native and it is even less likely to be a native

of a local coast-adapted community, say, in the county of Cornwall. In his excellent and thought-provoking *Bringing Nature Home*, Douglas Tallamy offers a far more useable definition by suggesting that "a plant can only function as a true native while it is interacting with the community that historically helped shape it."

For instance, while many garden plants, including numerous grasses, can act as nectar suppliers to bees and butterflies, far fewer are able to serve as (equally essential) breeding host facilities for many of our native insects, or indeed to supply food for the numerous leaf-chewers which over long periods of time have developed relationships with specific plants that were locally native. To be of such value to the garden's ecosystem, a plant must have a connection with the geographical area in which it is being planted; it has to be locally native.

Provenance, where a plant comes from, can be equally important

Vast expanses of locally native common reed, *Phragmites australis*, are havens for wildlife in the Neretva Delta in Croatia. When introduced in the United States, where *P. a.* is also native, this European form proved substantially less valuable to wildlife than its American counterpart. Photograph courtesy of Amanda Walker.

Native plants bring a sense of time-lessness and belonging to our gardens and designed spaces. On Ferndown Common, Dorset, England, during a heavy frost the purple moor grass, *Molinia caerulea* (above, middleground), appears in perfect harmony with its surroundings, creating a visually stunning master-piece that is also a fully function-ing part of the local biodiversity.

Plants that are native to an area are often the best choices for specific tasks that mirror their natural surround-ings. The common reed, *Phragmites australis* (right), is ideally suited for use in stabilizing steep banks or other areas prone to slip, as it is supremely adept at colonizing similar areas in its natural environment.

to a plant's biodiversity value. The common reed, *Phragmites australis*, is native to both Europe and the United States—but when the European form was introduced in America, it was found to sustain a much smaller insect population than the locally native form, despite being identical to the human eye. Cultivar selection, the process of encouraging ornamental qualities to gradually enhance the gardenworthy aspects of a native grass, does not appear to denude the grasses' value as locally functioning natives.

WHY NATIVES?   Grasses are present in just about every natural system in virtually every part of the world. While not all native grasses are gardenworthy, they offer numerous opportunities for gardeners to choose plants that have not only ornamental qualities but also a geographical connection to the area of their intended use. What's more, using natives that have adapted and evolved in the local area removes the risk of gardeners introducing exotic escapees (more weeds), simply as those plants will have already been present as natives. When we accept the principle of 'right plant, right place', it is a short step to the appreciation that plants already thriving in the surrounding area are likely best adapted to the local climatic conditions, and therefore make the sensible, informed choice for garden use.

For purely aesthetic reasons, well-chosen and thoughtfully used native plantings can create an unparalleled sense of place, a sense of belonging that is almost impossible to emulate with an eclectic palette of plants chosen, however carefully, from different areas of the world.

Another (and perhaps the single most valuable) argument for using more native plants in our gardens is that they are more readily accepted as food, shelter and living space by a much greater percentage of the birds, insects and animals that, along with plants, make up the balance of the local communities—the biodiversity upon which all things ultimately depend. While at first glance our individual domestic gardens may seem relatively insignificant, while the amount of wild and natural space declines at a frighteningly rapid pace, our gardens play an increasingly essential role in the future wellbeing of our plant, insect and animal life.

EIGHT
Looking After Grasses

GRASSES ARE GENUINELY easy to look after. With a little annual attention, they will generously repay in the form of a very long display that is as short on work as it is high on value. Tuning in to what your grasses need, and planning accordingly, will make things easier still.

Routine Maintenance

In caring for grasses, the annual routine will depend very much on whether the grasses are deciduous or evergreen. Because grasses can resent disturbance during the dormant winter months, most tasks are best carried out from early spring onwards, when the worst of the winter weather has passed and the plants are beginning to break into growth. As a general rule, very few of the usual tasks often associated with garden plants, such as staking and deadheading, are necessary with grasses. While individual circumstance may dictate some mid-season treatment, for the most part grasses will be happy with attention just once a year.

The first few weeks after being cut back are the least interesting for deciduous grasses, but in only a matter of days new growth begins to appear. In the meantime, a decorative mulch such as the gravel and boulders used here at the RHS Garden Wisley in Surrey, England provides early contrast for the emerging green shoots of African lovegrass, *Eragrostis curvula*.

DECIDUOUS GRASSES Deciduous grasses are those whose stems last only one year, producing a new sheaf of growth at the start of each season. The deciduous types, which include many of the true grasses we see in gardens, including *Miscanthus*, *Molinia*, *Panicum*, *Pennisetum* and *Eragrostis*, stop growing and shut down for the winter in temperate climates. In common with many other perennials, grasses have the ability to retain their stems and flowers virtually intact, gradually drying and changing colour through myriad subtle tones of brown and beige in tune with the seasons. It is largely this ability to retain the dried outline of stem, leaf and flower that gives grasses such a long season of interest in the garden.

For deciduous types, the annual routine consists of simply removing the old dried stems to prepare for the new season's rapid growth. Under natural conditions, this removal is accomplished through a combination of elements including wind and fire; in the garden, this role is more conveniently undertaken by the gardener. Where a more natural look is desired, this annual routine could be applied less frequently.

Cutting back can be achieved by a variety of different tools, from hand-held scissors to motorized flail mowers. It is chiefly a question of convenience for the user, though undoubtedly mechanized trimmers are more efficient for larger areas. Removal of stems close to ground level allows for the new growth to show through quickly, while cutting through any existing new growth in the process of taking off the old does no harm to the plant.

Subsequent disposal of the cut stems is also largely a matter of personal preference. The old stems can be physically removed from the area to be composted, or burned, or they can be left in situ to be used as labour-saving mulch. To create a practical and pleasing mulch layer, the stems will need reducing into much smaller pieces, either by initially chopping into smaller sections if using shears or trimmers or by running a rough rotary grass cutter over the areas once cut down. The cut stems can also be passed through a garden shredder to create a fine mulch, and flail mowers can be a useful alternative for larger unobstructed areas where the flailing action cuts and macerates the old growth in one simple operation.

Which maintenance tool to use is a matter of personal preference. Mechanical or electric trimmers are certainly faster, while hand tools can offer a greater degree of control for more delicate tasks.

The old stems are cut back as close to ground level as is practical, leaving a light and airy base from which new shoots will emerge.

Shorter-handled trimmers are sometimes more adept at cutting around finer growth.

All cut growth should be removed from the crown either by hand or rake and can subsequently be composted, chipped, burned or simply left in place as a mulch.

In agricultural situations, a long-established alternative to cutting is the controlled burning of old growth, mimicking the cycle of some natural systems. While undoubtedly effective in skilled hands, this option is potentially very hazardous, especially within the confines of a garden setting, and is not normally recommended (see page 59).

The 'Chelsea Chop' is a technique that can reduce the ultimate height of fast-growing deciduous grasses, and some perennials, that regularly become too tall for a given situation. Cutting the new growth back to the ground is carried out in late May, around the time of the famous Flower Show, and reduces the amount of time the stems have to grow before flowering is initiated, thus reducing the overall height of the plant. Although it involves extra work, this can be an effective technique in certain situations (for instance, where very rich soils regularly create fast green growth that is inclined to flop later in the season).

SUMMER-DORMANT GRASSES   Summer-dormant grasses are often found in mediterranean areas. With respect to maintenance they are very similar to winter-dormant grasses in that old stems are cut down, if desired, at some point during dormancy: either late in the season to enable enjoyment of the strawy silhouettes, or earlier in the season to reduce possible fire risk in sensitive areas.

EVERGREEN GRASSES   Caring for evergreen grasses is slightly more complex than maintaining the deciduous group. For at least the first season or two after planting, evergreens will need virtually no attention. However, the appearance of many finer-leaved evergreens such as *Nassella* and *Festuca* is improved by combing or raking through the foliage and removing much of the old, tired or dead leaves and flowers. Even domestic rubber gloves can be useful as debris will adhere to their semi-adhesive surface when passed, comb-like, through the foliage.

Shorter-lived grasses like *Festuca* can become unkempt relatively quickly, while longer-lived plants such as many forms of *Carex* can last noticeably longer before needing attention. Cursory removal of dead leaves by hand or combing through is the easiest and preferred option as long as it is effective.

Evergreens often need very little attention in the early years. Combing through in the spring with a rake (above) or other toothed implement will keep *Nassella tenuissima* fresh for another season.

Evergreens such as *Festuca glauca* 'Elijah Blue' (left) can be cut back hard to remove old, tired growth but to minimize the risk of damage this should only be done once the plant has come into active growth in spring. Hand tools are often easiest for this task leaving a tidy ball, or 'hedgehog', which will produce new growth within a matter of days.

Pheasant grass, *Anemanthele lessoniana*, is a relatively short-lived plant, surviving for about 3–5 years before gradually losing vigour. Once the plant starts becoming 'strawy', cutting back old foliage during active growth can prolong its useful life, but allowing a seedling or two to survive is part of a natural progression that the gardener can use to advantage.

Where this no longer has the desired results evergreens can be cut back, quite hard in many cases, but in most temperate climates this should only be carried out while the plants are in active growth. Hard pruning stimulates new growth from the base, but evergreens can take severe exception to being heavily pruned, especially when in dormancy. Cutting back during active growth minimizes this risk by stimulating an almost immediate response in the form of new shoots.

The extent to which old foliage is removed often depends on a combination of the garden conditions, individual plants and personal experience of what works best. Removal of between a third to a half of the old foliage on grasses such as *Anemanthele lessoniana* is a safe option in most areas, whereas taking the plant almost to ground level can also work successfully, especially in warmer climates with good light levels.

Festucas and many other finer-leaved evergreens will take a tighter pruning on an annual basis; after being cut back to a rounded mound early in the season, they quickly put on vigorous new growth. These quick-growing evergreens can be cut back at almost any point during the active growing period as they will start regrowth quickly—sometimes within hours of being trimmed.

SEMI-EVERGREEN GRASSES   While evergreen in more favourable climates, semi-evergreen grasses, such as *Elymus* and *Helictotrichon,* can frequently become effectively deciduous by the end of the winter period. On the whole this group will tolerate being cut back to a tight mound, or even to the ground, on a regular basis, provided that the plants have begun active growth.

Advice for Maintaining Meadows, Lawns and Green Roofs

Many of the evergreen grasses and sedges that are used in low-maintenance lawns and meadows can be cut at any time during the growing season, per the grasses' normal recommendations. In warmer climates the acceptable cutting time can include most of the rainy winter period, especially for cool-season plants.

Lawns made from slow-growing sedges such as *Carex praegracilis* can be either left entirely uncut, cut once annually to freshen growth, or cut on a weekly basis with a regular lawn mower for a smoother, finer finish. The regime depends very much on the effect that is required.

The 'No Maintenance' Option?

There is no such thing as 'no maintenance' in a garden situation but there can be varying degrees of low maintenance that come close. In nature, 'pruning' and 'cutting back' are only enacted by a combination of wind, animals and other physical agencies; otherwise, the grasses lose old growth that either gradually breaks away or is covered by emerging new growth. Perfectly adapted as this process is in our natural systems, under garden conditions, often with less well-balanced plant communities, the results of such an approach can appear messy and unworkable.

Mulching and Feeding

Renowned for their general ability to grow in nutrient-poor soils in the wild, grasses' natural fastidiousness is carried over to garden conditions, where almost all grasses will require very little to no feeding.

Indeed, in extreme circumstances it is possible to overfeed grasses to the detriment of flower in favour of foliage, and using grasses from nutrient-poor areas in high-nutrient garden soils can result in a similar alteration to the plants' growth habit. In practice, however, this is not usually a major concern although in some situations—for instance, when carrying out habitat restoration work or in other sensitive areas— nutrient levels may be an issue.

Mulching, the laying of an organic or inorganic material on top of soil and around plants, is recommended practice in most garden situations. Mulch material is usually bark, garden compost, manure, spent hops or other organic material, though the use of stone and gravel and other inorganic substances such as crushed brick rubble should not be overlooked. The depth to which a mulch should be applied is often a matter of preference and material availability, but generally 25–50 mm (1–2 inches) is a workable guideline. To be most effective the mulch should cover the entire planting area (not just to the area immediately adjacent to the plants), though care should be taken to avoid covering the crowns of the plants as this may lead to rotting. If the old growths of deciduous grasses are cut and left in situ, this in itself provides a self-sustaining mulch with very little effort from the gardener.

Aesthetic considerations and a reduced need to weed are two main reasons for applying mulches, though it could be argued that the single most important reason is that of water conservation. A mulch helps to retain moisture in the soil over an extended period, much to the advantage of young, thirsty roots that are prone to drying out in the early stages of life.

Looking After Container-Grown Grasses

With their fibrous root systems, so many grasses lend themselves easily to pot and container growth. Annual routines for pot-grown grasses do not differ from those grown in the ground, except that the pot-grown grasses' root systems will demand more regular attention.

With vigorous root systems an annual potting of all but the

As with most other plants in containers, grasses' roots will outgrow the available space—sometimes in one season in the case of vigorous plants such as *Pennisetum alopecuroides* 'Hameln', whose roots have here formed a dense ball in the outline of its container. For continued healthy, vigorous growth the roots need a regular supply of new soil. Where it is impractical to pot on into a larger container, cutting back and removing roots by approximately $\frac{1}{3}$ from the bottom allows new soil to be placed in the existing container. Finally, replacing the top section of the plant on the new compost ensures a fresh root run for another growing season. This technique can be repeated on an annual basis, time after time, though the plant will eventually require division to maintain vigour.

slowest-growing grasses such as *Hakonechloa* is usually necessary. If roots slow down, inevitably the top growth will follow, leading quickly to disappointing performance and senescence. Potting on into a larger container each year is a simple procedure using any well-balanced potting medium, though eventually it becomes impractical to pot into a yet larger container; while dividing the plant solves this issue, it also reduces the size of the plant left for display. Where a mature size is desired, removing the bottom third or even half of the old rootball in spring, along with a section of the side growth if necessary, and replacing it with fresh growing medium allows for the plant to be replaced intact in the old container, where it will grow with renewed vigour with its roots in contact with the fresh soil. This technique can be repeated on a regular basis until the plant's width demands division.

Planting and Renewal

With such a diverse group as the grasses, which successfully colonize under almost every conceivable climatic condition, there is no one perfect time for planting. It is often said among gardeners that while spring is the preferred period for people to plant, autumn is nature's favourite time. Both can be true; there is no better way to determine the optimum planting time than consulting local practices and tuning in to the surrounding conditions.

In the relatively mild dampness of maritime climates like that of the U.K., most times of year can be suitable for planting. In the mediterranean climate of California, on the other hand, planting after the onset of the first winter rains would likely be considered best practice. And yet in much of the United States, autumn planters are wary of 'frost heave', the process by which frost and ice pushes young plants out of the ground to the extent that spring may be considered the better choice.

PREPARATION   While choosing the right plants to suit the garden's conditions is no doubt the most important aspect of successful planting, ensuring that the soil is in suitable condition to receive those plants is arguably the second most important. Although grasses in particular

are tolerant of a wide range of cultural and soil conditions, common sense dictates that plants finding themselves in properly aerated, weed-free conditions will establish more successfully than those that have to fight for their survival from the moment of planting.

Best practice under garden conditions involves ensuring the prior removal of unwanted plants including, critically, their root systems. Where soils have been heavily compacted, preventing the free movement of water and air through the soil, it is usually essential to break this compaction before continuing with any further preparation. Machinery with hydraulic arms attached to digging buckets is ideal for this task.

Depending on local conditions, buying and planting from late summer to winter means that the grasses will have their current season's growth intact, giving a clearer idea of the plant's shape and characteristics.

HOW MANY PLANTS?   Most experienced gardeners will have developed their instincts when it comes to deciding how many plants should fill a given area. But whatever your level of experience, it is often useful to have a strategy for dealing with larger areas.

Visualizing an area in terms of square metres or square yards can not only help to calculate the number of plants needed, but it can also aid in design and layout by crystallizing plant patterns and even plant choice. When you break up the planting area into square metres or square yards and consider how many plants will be needed per square, it becomes easier to plan plant density and anticipate the quantity that will be needed—which can be adjusted and re-calculated to allow for budgets or design considerations. (See the Appendices for recommended plant densities.)

PROPAGATION AND RENEWAL Grasses are propagated either by seed or through division. For annuals, seed sowing is the only option—and in addition to being relatively cheap, it is the time-honoured way to ensure genetic diversity among the different species.

Division, the splitting up of a mature plant into smaller pieces, is used for cultivars or those plants that will not necessarily retain their unique characteristics if reproduced from seed. It is also the most convenient method in garden situations where the lifting and dividing of an existing plant rejuvenates that plant at the same time as providing a ready supply of new plants for little cost or effort.

Deciduous grasses are ideally lifted and split in early spring, just as they are breaking into growth. The evergreens can be divided at the same time, though in many cooler climates it is best to delay until the plant is actively growing. Evergreens can also be split at virtually any time during active growth in the summer.

A few grasses do not take kindly to division. One example is the pheasant grass, *Anemanthele lessoniana*, which is best raised from seed. Others like *Stipa gigantea,* the Spanish oat grass, can also object to unnecessary disturbance. In such cases, best results are usually achieved by dividing the plant while it is still in the ground, cutting off and lifting smaller sections with a sharp spade while still leaving the majority of the plant undisturbed in the ground.

Nearly all grasses can set seed in favourable circumstances—some, such as the shorter-lived grasses, more easily than others. This seed can be collected while still on the plant in the early autumn and stored in

paper envelopes or bags in a cool dry place until spring, when it can be sown under controlled conditions much as with any other ornamental plant. (As a general rule, seed collected from garden cultivars will not usually come true to type, so cultivars should not be propagated by seed.)

Where the seed is not collected, or eaten during the winter months by other inhabitants of the garden, some may germinate in the spring. Applying an early mulch controls unwanted grass seed as it would any other type of seed. You can use any unwanted resultant seedlings as a stock to replace old plants or as a fresh supply for new plantings. Sowing directly onto prepared ground can work well, especially with annuals, but in a garden setting (where conditions are not controlled) results for most grasses will vary and success is not guaranteed.

When planting larger areas, thinking in terms of plants per square metre or square yard can help to crystallize ideas of planting patterns and even the plant palette.

While requiring only the annual removal of dead stems for many years, most deciduous grasses will eventually benefit from division and renewal. The timespan for this depends mostly on planting conditions and the species involved. This miscanthus, while still healthy after 8 years in the ground undisturbed, has begun to show a marked dead space in the centre which is not producing the same level of new growth that can be seen on the outside of the plant once it has been lifted (top right). A simple division by spade is enough to re-energize the plant, replanting or discarding the newly split sections as needed (bottom right).

Pests and Diseases

On the whole grasses are remarkably free from disease, with only foliar rusts appearing regularly. Frequently resulting from cultural conditions, these rusts are usually only temporary and are easy enough to ignore in all but the most delicate of situations where a chemical solution may be employed. Alternatively, cutting back the foliage to encourage fresh new growth is often easier than resorting to chemicals, which should only be used in extreme circumstances.

SUCKERS   While grasses can play host to a variety of sucking insects such as aphids, in general they are relatively free from all but the most extreme infestations. When infestation by sucking insect occurs, physical removal or spraying can be undertaken if you prefer not to let nature take its course.

Most forms of *Carex* can suffer from aphids, which colonize the leaf bases and root systems of the plant, remaining almost invisible in the dense foliage or below ground. More often seen in pot-grown plants, a lack of vigour characterizes a severe attack, which can be dealt with through chemical treatment or physical removal.

One species of mealybug, *Miscanthicoccus miscanthi*, has been a recent pest of *Miscanthus* (especially in the United States), causing stunted growth and a twisting of flowerheads. Difficult to spot in the early stages, chemical control or disposal of infected plants are the usual solutions.

GRAZERS AND BURROWERS   A wide range of grazing animals will choose grasses as food sources. Most, such as deer, rabbits and a selection of rodents—not to mention, on a smaller scale, domestic cats and dogs—browse the top growth. Still others such as voles, gophers and moles burrow underground where they eat the root systems and frequently cause severe damage and death to the plants attacked.

The browsing animals' tastes vary, with regional differences sometimes emerging so that, for example, panicums may be unpalatable in one area only to become a favoured food item in another. No reliably browser-proof grasses seem to exist, and physical prevention or control of the animals involved appear the only viable options when the damage becomes unacceptable. Planting larger quantities of the same plant can allow for a higher level of damage before aesthetic considerations are compromised.

NINE
Directory of Grasses and Grass-like Plants

Rushes are round,
sedges have edges
and grasses have nodes
from the top to the ground.
　　—from an oft-quoted ditty

AMONG THE GRASSES and grass-like plants described here, you will find choices that are ornamental, as well as some with biodiversity value, others that play a part in erosion control, and quite a few with all of these traits. With more than ten thousand different species of grasses existing today, as well as over three thousand species of sedges alone—not to mention many other allied species and innumerable garden selections—it would have been impossible to include all of them. Instead, I describe a carefully chosen and wide-ranging selection of plants that, in some way or another, bring value to the garden.

You can simply browse this Directory for something eye-catching, or look up a specific plant that has caught your interest in the past. In each entry, I have tried to shed light on whether a given plant is likely to thrive in your garden and how you might use it to best effect.

The Decennium border at Knoll
Gardens is at its most resplendent
in September and October.

Clump-Formers, Runners and Seeders

When choosing a grass, it is useful to understand how it will 'behave' in the garden. From a gardener's perspective, grasses and grass-like plants can be categorized according to how they spread. There are those whose roots form effectively stationary clumps, and others whose roots travel or otherwise spread through the soil. Finally, there are the annual grasses that reproduce exclusively from seed.

CLUMP-FORMERS   The clump-formers, also known as bunch grasses, generally have the best garden manners in that their fibrous root systems produce relatively tight clumps of stems that will never stray very far from the original planting position. Over a period of time these clumps can attain significant size, sometimes eventually dying out in the congested centre as sometimes happens with pampas and *Miscanthus*, but they can be rejuvenated by lifting and dividing whenever necessary almost ad infinitum.

RUNNERS   The runners are those whose roots move through the soil away from the original planting position, frequently with the ability to cover large areas of ground over a short period of time. These root systems are a successful adaptation for grasses like the marram grass,

A fibrous root system (below) leads to clump-forming plants like this miscanthus. Clump-formers make ideal garden plants, as while they may gain considerable size and width, they never stray far from their original planting position.

Grasses with running root systems (right), such as the common reed, can become a nuisance under the controlled conditions of a garden or border—but they are ideal for use in lawns and green roofs and for erosion control, where their wandering roots help to stabilize soils and sands.

so often seen on sandy beaches where the ability to move around is advantageous. Grasses with these continually questing roots can more easily outstay their welcome in the relatively controlled conditions of a garden; however, for applications such as lawns and green roofs, where a close carpet of growth is required, having a mobile and self-renewing root system becomes a distinct advantage.

Some plants that are widely regarded as being clump-forming technically have spreading roots, but spread so comparatively slowly so that from a horticultural standpoint they can usually be regarded as clump-formers. For example, most miscanthus are regarded as clump-forming, but *Miscanthus sacchariflorus* has the ability to spread, though in most climates it makes only moderately spreading patches which, to a gardener's eyes, can be seen as rather large clumps. It is only in warmer climates that this spreading ability becomes more pronounced.

SEEDERS   Like most other plants, grasses will seed given the right conditions. However it is really the annuals and ephemerals (those with lifespans of under one year) that make up this third group: the seeders.

By definition, an annual must set seed to survive; the more copious the seed produced, the better the chances of success. Such free-seeding annuals can outstay their welcome in the garden and should be introduced with appropriate caution. Some, like *Setaria macrostachya*, are light and delicate despite producing copious seedlings and, with timely editing, will not necessarily upset the balance with other plants, at least in cooler areas.

Warm-Season or Cool-Season?

Across most of the plant world, the terms 'warm-season growers' and 'cool-season growers' are used to describe basic technical differences between how plants obtain their energy. Complicated in detail, these differences can be important from a gardener's point of view in that warm-season grasses such as *Arundo*, *Eragrostis*, *Miscanthus* and *Pennisetum* are at their best in warm conditions. They tend to start into growth relatively late in the season and are capable of doing so speedily when soil conditions and air temperatures are warm and to their liking.

Contrastingly, cool-season grasses such as *Calamagrostis*, *Festuca*, *Milium* and *Stipa* fare better at cooler temperatures, will start into growth much earlier in the spring and are frequently at their best when conditions are moister, usually in late winter to spring.

Sun or Shade? Wet or Dry?

In nature plants are mostly adapted to specific conditions such as sun or shade, wet or dry, and this general advice is given in the descriptions. This tendency to adapt, however, is a constantly evolving, dynamic process and in practice most plants have a range of tolerances that the gardener can use to advantage. For example, *Carex secta* is happy in sun and under wet conditions, where it makes a magnificent dark green mound. But under much drier conditions in some shade it can still perform satisfactorily, though perhaps not as exuberantly. As with all living things, experimentation is key to success.

Hardiness Zones

A plant's tolerances extend to its ability to cope with widely differing temperature regimes. In the following entries, Hardiness Zones are given as a guide as to how a plant may perform. Zone numbers refer to the lowest cold-hardiness zone in which the plant is likely to survive.

Local weather conditions, soils, and microclimate are all likely to have a substantial impact on a plant's hardiness and due weight must be given to these other factors when evaluating whether a plant is likely to be hardy in your garden. For more information on Hardiness Zones, and to calculate your Zone based on your area's minimum temperature, please refer to page 257.

Maximum Heights, Planting Densities and Lifespans

The maximum heights given in these descriptions refer to the ultimate statures generally achievable under average-to-good conditions. This height includes the flowers, which typically make up a significant part of a grass's overall height. For example, *Stipa gigantea* is listed as being up to 2.4 m (8 ft.) tall when in full flower, although the basal foliage itself is less than half that height.

In poor conditions or where a plant is at the edge of its tolerances, this maximum height might be reduced by up to one third. Maximum heights are approximate; the height that a specific plant will achieve depends on the specific conditions in the garden.

When planning the garden, the distance that should be left between plants can vary quite significantly depending on the size and vigour of the plants themselves, the soil conditions and the desired effect. For suggestions on planting densities, please turn to page 260.

As with any other diverse group, grasses' lifespans vary tremendously. They range from the annuals, which last a season, through short-lived perennials that can be expected to live anywhere from two to five years, to the long-haul perennial grasses that live for ten years and often much longer.

The Naming of Plants

The naming of plants, or plant nomenclature, is an often complex and confusing subject that is well beyond the scope of this book. Modern identification techniques are providing results that can challenge long-held traditional views, with taxonomists suggesting a plethora of name changes that are not always welcome to the gardener unconcerned with the background science. My approach to naming plants, in this Directory and throughout the book, is purely intended to match plants with widely accepted names and should not be taken as an opinion on the botanical validity of those names used.

If a plant's scientific name appears to be missing from this alphabetical listing, it may be because the name has been changed by taxonomists. To find the current name, look up the 'missing' name in the Index. Cultivar names are enclosed by single quotation marks and any synonyms for cultivars follow the current name and are enclosed in parentheses. Unless otherwise indicated, cultivars can be assumed to share the approximate maximum height and frost-hardiness of the species under which they are classified.

Achnatherum

NEEDLE GRASS, SPIKE GRASS

Originally classified under *Stipa*, these cool-season deciduous ornamental grasses are clump forming. *Achnatherum* species take their common name from the needle-like characteristics of their flowers.

Achnatherum calamagrostis

SILVER SPEAR GRASS

Formerly well-known as *Stipa calamagrostis*, this long-established grass is deservedly popular for its dense clumps of bright green foliage that host numerous subtly arching stems weighted by freely produced needle-like flowers to create a wonderfully light and feathery appearance. Compact in habit and very useful at the front of border plantings or as a low informal hedge as well as in drifts and larger masses where it excels. Very tolerant of drought, sunshine and poor soils but less happy under warm, humid conditions. Dislikes being crowded by other plants. From Europe. To 90 cm (3 ft.). Z5.

'Lemperg'. A little more compact but with the same free-flowering nature.

Achnatherum coronatum

syn *Stipa coronata*

GIANT NEEDLE GRASS

Of limited range, this dramatic species prefers sun-baked, dry, gravelly soils and produces tall upward-pointing flower stems from tight clumps during spring. From California and Mexico. To 1.8 m (6 ft.). Z7.

Achnatherum calamagrostis

Achnatherum extremiorientale

syn *Stipa extremiorientale*

EASTERN NEEDLE GRASS

An unassuming choice, with tall, light, airy panicles coming from clumps of mid-green leaves. Prefers not-too-dry soils in sun or light shade. From China, Japan and Siberia. To 1.5 m (5 ft.). Z5.

Achnatherum hymenoides

syn *Oryzopsis hymenoides*

INDIAN RICE GRASS, SILKY GRASS

An early food crop throughout the western United States where it is palatable to livestock, this clump-forming plant produces fine-textured airy flowers with moisture quickly drying to make a silky-looking rounded silhouette. Very sun- and drought-tolerant, disliking too much moisture under garden conditions. From North America. To 60 cm (2 ft.). Z5.

Acorus

SWEET FLAG

Although not botanically true grass, this useful group of grass-like evergreens has narrow iris-like evergreen foliage that is slowly spreading, tough and long lived. *Acorus calamus*, the sweet flag, is even more iris-like; *Acorus gramineus* is the most widely used in gardens.

Acorus gramineus

Produces compact, tightly formed clumps of evergeen foliage that can slowly attain more bulk over time. Found in damp to wet waterside conditions, this small species has given rise to many cultivars usually distinguished primarily by leaf colouration. From Japan, India and China. To 30 cm (1 ft.). Z5–7.

'Ogon'. The most widespread cultivar, with bright gold-, yellow-, green- and even cream-striped leaves forming typical slowly spreading mounds. Leaf colouration can vary markedly, due perhaps to differing seasonal or even cultural conditions, leading to speculation as to whether the form now commonly grown is in fact the original correctly named plant. Regardless, 'Ogon' is reliable for damp areas but will also survive happily under drier conditions such as in containers.

'Variegatus'. Slow-growing but attractive, with creamy white and grey-green narrow evergreen foliage that can be slightly pendulous towards the tips.

Agrostis

BENT GRASS

A genus of widely occurring and diverse cool-season deciduous grasses, *Agrostis* contains more than two hundred annual and perennial species, some being used as components of lawn grass. Originates from a widespread area, especially northern-hemisphere temperate climates.

Acorus gramineus 'Variegatus'

Agrostis nebulosa

syn *Agrostis capillaris*
CLOUD GRASS

A pretty annual with an apt common name. Covers itself in the most delicate, airy flowerheads. Like most annuals, it is quick growing and prefers generally open sunny conditions. Re-sows if happy. From Spain, Morocco and Portugal. To 30 cm (1 ft.). Z5–7.

Alopecurus

FOXTAIL

Alopecurus consists of cool-season deciduous grasses, both annuals and perennials. Not of major importance in gardens, foxtails are mostly a constituent of pasture and other grassy areas. The common name refers to the cylindrical flowerheads produced early in the season.

Alopecurus pratensis 'Variegatus'

GOLDEN MEADOW FOXTAIL

Although naturalized over large areas of North America, the species is most commonly seen in this attractive golden-foliaged form, which is brightest at flowering time and in full sun. Old growth can be cut back to encourage fresh growth after flowering ends. From Eurasia. To 60 cm (2 ft.). Z4.

Ammophila

MARRAM, BEACH GRASS, DUNE GRASS

Confined to coastal sand dunes, these salt-tolerant, warm-season deciduous beach grasses have highly adapted fast-moving root systems that have made them essential elements in the control and stabilization of sand dunes. Successfully used in restoration and erosion control schemes where the European species has been used outside of its own natural range, it has been found to outcompete and displace native beach grasses.

Ammophila arenaria

MARRAM, EUROPEAN BEACH GRASS

A coast-hugging species whose rapidly spreading, aggressive nature makes it excellent for stabilizing sand dunes. Has tough grey-green foliage and strongly upright buff flowerheads. Often seen in association with *Leymus* from which it can be differentiated by its smaller leaves and distinct clumping appearance. From Europe and North Africa. To 90 cm (3 ft.). Z5.

Ammophila breviligulata

AMERICAN BEACH GRASS

A cousin to the European dune grass—and similar in many respects, being an essential stabilizer on coastal sand dunes. Several selections such as 'Cape' and 'Hattersas' have been made for their regionally adapted qualities. From coastal eastern U.S. To 90 cm (3 ft.). Z5.

Ampelodesmos

Ampelodesmos consists of a single species of clump-forming, warm-season evergreen grass whose foliage superficially resembles that of pampas grass. Once used for tying vines.

Ampelodesmos mauritanicus

VINE REED, ROPE GRASS

Imposing mounds of tough evergreen foliage support tall pale stems of striking one-sided drooping flowerheads, creating a distinctive outline in the best forms, which can vary considerably as most production is from seed. Requires a sunny well-drained position to do well. From North Africa and mediterranean Europe. To 2.4 m (8 ft.). Z7–8.

Andropogon

BEARDGRASS

A large and wide-ranging group including some of the best-known and most numerous prairie grasses, all warm-season deciduous. A much smaller number of cultivated species are valuable clump-forming garden plants, generally upright in habit with stems and leaves offering a wide selection of warm oranges, cinnamons and reds especially during autumn. Originates from tropical and temperate climates.

Andropogon gerardii

BIG BLUESTEM, TURKEY FOOT

'Turkey foot' describes the shape of the often 'three-toed' flowers appearing atop the elegant tall stems in a range of subtle colours ranging from green to almost blue—perhaps the plant's strongest feature, especially when used in large groups and in association with other perennials. The tallest and perhaps most distinctive of prairie grasses, *A. g.* has produced many noteworthy cultivars that accentuate its vertical habit and ability to provide spectacular autumnal pageants of colour. Long-lived, tough and hardy in wet to dry soils. Requires open sunny conditions for best performance. Under garden conditions, too rich a soil or shade will incline the plants towards toppling, just as they should be at their best. From North America, including Mexico. To 2.4 m (8 ft.). Z3.

'Lord Snowden's Big Blue'. An especially

Ampelodesmos mauritanicus. Photograph courtesy of Dianna Jazwinski.

Andropogon gerardii. Photograph courtesy of Dianna Jazwinski.

upright selection that combines possibly the tallest and bluest of stems and leaves though still offering purple hues during cooler autumn days.

'New Wave'. A striking selection from seed, with strong reddish stems that are distinctly upright, holding the flowers quite clear of purple-tinged clumps of green foliage. To 1.8 m (6 ft.).

Andropogon glomeratus

syn *Andropogon virginicus* var. *abbreviatus*.
BUSHY BEARDGRASS
Naturally occurs in wet places like marshes and bogs, with relatively short though still upright flower stems that are noticeably fluffy when in seed. The stiff stems of *A. g.* var. *scabriglumis* are a little taller; limited to warmer areas, it is not quite as hardy. Both make excellent garden plants, especially in prairie or meadow plantings, preferring full sun. From North America. To 90 cm (3 ft.). Z5.

Andropogon virginicus

BROOMSEDGE
Tough and adaptable, occurring over a wide area and under greatly differing soil conditions. Especially valuable when used en masse such as in meadows where its bright autumnal and winter colourations, ranging from almost bright orange to dull copper, create the most striking of effects. At its best in poor soils and full sun. From North America. To 90 cm (3 ft.). Z3.

Andropogon virginicus var. *glaucus*

CHALKY BLUESTEM
Less cold-hardy but more heat tolerant than *A. v.*, this geographically limited variety is distinct for its glaucous blue summer foliage that has given rise to several cultivars with more intense blue colourations. Especially useful in drought-prone areas in full sun. From the southern U.S. To 90 cm (3 ft.). Z7.

Anemanthele

Native to both North and South Islands of New Zealand from hilltop to sea level, this genus comprises just one species of ornamental cool-season evergreen grass—long known to gardeners as *Stipa arundinacea*.

Anemanthele lessoniana

syn *Stipa arundinacea*, *Oryzopsis lessoniana*.
PHEASANT TAIL, WIND GRASS
A most graceful and useful clump-forming evergreen that happily tolerates a range of conditions from full sun to fairly deep shade with apparent equanimity, even surviving under the canopy of established trees in the driest of conditions. Happy also in most soils except wet, this is one of the very few true grasses to accept such wide-ranging sunlight levels and as a result is much valued by gardeners, especially for dry shade. Forming extremely graceful mounds of leaves gently cascading from a central tight clump that does not split easily, the leaves follow a constantly changing pattern of greens, tans, oranges and reds, though in deepest shade they tend to remain green. Easy to establish. Masses of tiny pinkish red flowers on lax stems are produced profusely enough to cover the plant in a gauzy cascade of pink. Will re-seed but does not appear to be ecologically invasive. To 75 cm ($2\frac{1}{2}$ ft.). Z8.

'Gold Hue'. A seldom-seen selected form, displaying a lighter yellowy gold foliage colour for a much longer period of time.

Aristida

THREE AWN
A very large and wide-ranging group of warm-season deciduous, mostly clump-forming bunch grasses, often a major constituent of dry grasslands such as savannah in North America, Africa, Asia and Australasia.

Aristida purpurea

PURPLE THREE AWN

A common element of Californian dry grass-lands, named for its flowers which are produced in some profusion over a long period. Can provide a vivid sense of drama when used in sufficient quantities such as in a meadow planting or large drifts. Bright green bunches of leaves support the flowers for the earlier part of the year with stems, leaves and flowers all gradually drying and bleaching during dry summers, though in coastal areas it may stay active all season. Re-seeds easily under the right conditions. Tolerates a wide variety of soils though mostly dry and always requiring full sun. From the southern U.S. To 60 cm (2 ft.). Z6.

Arrhenatherum

OAT GRASS

Includes four species of cool-season deciduous grasses inclined towards weediness.

Arrhenatherum elatius subsp. *bulbosum* 'Variegatum'

ONION COUCH

A seldom-encountered older cultivar that forms neat mounds of white-and-darker-green-striped leaves with the white predominant enough to give an almost-white appearance overall. Best in cool areas, the foliage can appear shabby at times though cutting back the old growth will stimulate a fresh crop of brighter coloured leaves. Plant in an open sunny position for best effect, though in warmer climates some shade may return best results. From Africa, Asia and Eurasia. To 45 cm ($1\frac{1}{2}$ ft.). Z4.

Arundo

REED

Only three species comprise this small but well-known group of warm-season semi-evergreen grasses. All have a running rootstock and can be mistaken for bamboos at a casual glance.

Anemanthele lessoniana

Arundo donax

Arundo donax 'Versicolor'

Arundo donax

GIANT REED

Despite having naturalized over a wide area, especially in warmer climates where there is sufficient moisture to fuel its phenomenal rate of growth and sunlight to allow it to set fertile seed, the giant reed remains a valuable garden plant in areas where its vigour is at least partially restrained by climatic conditions. Tall, strongly upright stems and long grey-green leaves tapering to a point make it the biggest grass, reaching around 5 m (15 ft.) in warm areas where it remains evergreen. In cooler climates the stems and leaves become so bedraggled after winter that it is best cut to ground level when it can still reach heights of 3–4 m (10–14 ft.) in a single season. Not picky about soil conditions, it will tolerate various levels of drought and moisture and while aggressively colonizing in the warmest areas is content to make slowly spreading, though still large, clumps in colder areas. Always prefers sun. From Africa, Asia and Eurasia. Z6.

'Golden Chain'. A golden-variegated form with the same striking patterns as 'Versicolor' but with a less robust growth rate and even less cold-hardy. Needs sun and shelter. To 2.4 m (8 ft.). Z8.

'Macrophylla'. An excellent garden form that has wider and greyer leaves, and thicker stems that are almost vertical and not nearly so tall. As hardy as the species. To 2.7 m (9 ft.).

'Versicolor' ('Variegata'). Possibly among the most beautiful of variegated plants, with large wide leaves and stout stems all strikingly striped in creamy white and green and occasionally marbled with many shades of pink. Noticeably less hardy than the type, it will need some protection over winter in colder areas. To 2.4 m (8 ft.). Z8.

Arundo formosana

TAIWAN GRASS

Smaller in all parts than the giant reed, this downsized version has a daintiness absent from the species. Forms tighter clumps than *A. donax*, with more regularly produced pink-suffused blooms. Not overly fussy about soil, but requires sun. From Asia. To 2.4 m (8 ft.). Z6.

'Green Fountain'. A selection from China with a more rounded form.

'Oriental Gold'. Very distinctive with bright green-and-yellow-striped foliage. Occasionally produces bright pink flowers.

Arundo plinii

syn *Arundo pliniana*

Arguably has less ornamental value than *A. formosana*, being noticeably shorter, strongly spreading and with sharply pointed leaves. Produces flowers only in areas with a long growing season and widely regarded as not very cold-hardy in garden situations. From Africa, Asia and Eurasia. To 2.1 m (7 ft.). Z6.

Austrostipa

AUSTRALIAN FEATHERGRASS

Until recently the group of semi-evergreen grasses comprising *Austrostipa* were regarded as members of *Stipa*. The separate genus identifies those native to Australia and New Zealand.

Austrostipa elegantissima

syn *Stipa elegantissima*

FEATHER SPEARGRASS

Extremely delicate-looking airy panicles of flower, drying silver, gradually accumulate on the plant. Leaves are sparse and often inrolled. Needs sun and well-drained soils. Can be grown as a semi-trailing pot specimen in colder climates. From Australasia. To 60 cm (2 ft.). Z8.

Austrostipa ramosissima

syn *Stipa ramosissima*

PILLAR OF SMOKE, PLUME GRASS

Called 'pillar of smoke' for its masses of delicate airy inflorescences that are produced over long periods from upright pillars of stems and light green foliage. Prefers sunny open sites with some soil moisture in its native range and will adapt to drier conditions and even tolerate some shade in warmer climates. From Australasia. To 2.4 m (8 ft.). Z8.

Baumea

TWIG RUSH

This small group of semi-aquatic and marginal sedges are warm-season evergreen plants.

Austrostipa elegantissima. Photograph courtesy of Dianna Jazwinski.

Baumea rubiginosa

syn *Machaerina rubiginosa*

SOFT TWIG RUSH

Gradually spreading clumps of upright rush-like foliage are easily contained in gardens when used in boggy areas or water features and can be grown successfully in tubs and containers in colder areas. The selected form *B. rubiginosa* 'Variegata' has bright yellow stripes along one edge. Prefers sunny, damp areas. From Australasia. To 45 cm (1½ ft.). Z7.

Bothriochloa

BEARDGRASS

The perennial warm-season deciduous grasses in this relatively small group are often used in agriculture and include some species with distinctive ornamental value. Widely distributed in temperate and tropical areas.

Bothriochloa barbinodis

syn *Andropogon barbinodis*

SILVER BEARDGRASS

A highly attractive bunch grass producing slender flower stalks topped with initially slender silvery white flowers that gradually dry and open with age. Prefers an open position and is reasonably drought tolerant. The relatively tall stems can be lax; planting in groups and drifts largely overcomes this tendency. From the southern U.S. to Mexico. To 1.2 m (4 ft.). Z7.

Bothriochloa bladhii

syn *Bothriochloa caucasica*

BEARDGRASS

Distinctly delicate-looking, forming clumps of narrow light green foliage which can turn quite deep red autumnal colours. Flower spikes consist of widely spaced good silvery red flowers creating a light and airy effect. Needs full sun and well-drained warm soils. From Asia and Africa. To 1.2 m (4 ft.). Z7.

Bouteloua

GRAMA GRASS

A dry-loving group of annual and perennial warm-season semi-evergreen to deciduous grasses, many important for forage, present in both North and South America in open grasslands including short grass prairie.

Bouteloua curtipendula

SIDE OATS GRAMA

Relatively erect and distinct-looking, with noticeably one-sided flowers, initially purplish and coming from generally upright stems. Can also have

Bothriochloa bladhii. Photograph courtesy of Dianna Jazwinski.

purplish maroon-tinted leaves. In cooler temperatures, it will need full sun. Extremely drought-tolerant. From North and South America. To 90 cm (3 ft.). Z4.

Bouteloua gracilis

BLUE GRAMA, MOSQUITO GRASS
Daintier than side oats, with maroon-purple flowers, gradually curling with age, arranged at right angles to the stem. When planted in quantity the effect is almost magical. Tolerates a wide range of conditions, always prefers sun and may stay evergreen with sufficient moisture. Tough and adaptable, it is a successful lawn substitute that can be mown to a height of a few inches or left as an effective unmown meadow. From the southern U.S. To 60 cm (2 ft.). Z3.

Briza

QUAKING GRASS
A genus of annual and perennial, temperate, cool-season semi-evergreen grasses grown principally for their spikelets of heart-shaped flowers. The annual *B. maxima*, with the largest flowers, is commonly grown but often regarded as a weed in gardens due to its generous production of viable seed.

Briza media

QUAKING GRASS, PEARL GRASS,
RATTLE GRASS, TOTTER GRASS
Late spring sees the arrival of dainty spikelets of this easygoing clump-forming grass. Tolerates a wide range of soils from wet heavy clay to light dry sand, but prefers reasonably sunny open conditions. Frequently found in meadows and easily adapts to garden use; when massed, it re-creates the meadow feel. Flowers are purple at first, dancing in the slightest breeze. Once dried, they rustle and rattle with the wind but do not generally persist through the winter period. If cut down early

enough in the season, they can re-shoot with a second flush of leaves and sometimes flower. From Eurasia. To 75 cm ($2\frac{1}{2}$ ft.). Z4.

'Golden Bee'. A recent selection, perhaps a little more compact than the species, with flowerheads of a distinctive golden hue as they mature. To 60 cm (2 ft.).

'Limouzi'. With blue-green foliage, this selection is perhaps slightly slower to flower than other quaking grasses.

'Russells'. A pretty variegated form with white-and-green-striped foliage that can be tinged pink at cooler temperatures. This colouring extends to the flower stem, making an attractive overall ensemble. Sets viable seed that reverts to the species.

Bouteloua gracilis

Briza media. Photograph courtesy of Dianna Jazwinski.

Briza media 'Golden Bee'

Briza media 'Russells'

Bromus

BROME

Admittedly of limited ornamental value in gardens, these cool-season deciduous grasses have individually attractive flowers. Widely distributed in northern-hemisphere temperate regions.

Bromus inermis

SMOOTH BROOM

Of European origin, though now naturalized in the United States through its use as a hay and fodder crop, this species is usually represented in gardens by *B. inermis* 'Skinner's Gold'. Preferring sun or light shade, this cultivar has bright-yellow-striped foliage early in the cooler parts of the year, though faltering with increasing summer heat. Cutting back the old leaves once they fade can stimulate a fresh crop of better-coloured foliage. To 90 cm (3 ft.). Z4.

Calamagrostis

REED GRASS

The large and diverse number of cool-season deciduous grasses in this group are distinguished by their usually upright, sometimes feather-like flowers that prefer generally moist to wet soils in full sun to part shade. Widely distributed in northern temperate Eurasia, the U.K. and North America.

Calamagrostis ×acutiflora

FEATHER REED GRASS

A naturally occurring if seldom seen hybrid between *C. epigejos* and *C. arundinacea*, mostly represented by *C. ×acutiflora* 'Karl Foerster', named after the famous German nurseryman. Tough and adaptable, most forms prefer open positions and will tolerate a wide range of soil moisture except very dry. Z4.

'Avalanche'. Has clear wide white bands down the centre of each leaf and makes healthy mounds of foliage which are topped by silvery tan plumes on strongly vertical stems. Will tolerate light shade. To 1.5 m (5 ft.).

'Eldorado'. Slightly less hardy than the type, with bright golden-yellow-and-green-striped leaves. Will take light shade. Flowers are perhaps less upright than other forms. To 1.5 m (5 ft.).

'Karl Foerster' ('Stricta'). One of the most popular and easily recognizable of grasses, with tall, firmly upright narrow flower stems that are unremarkable individually but are packed together in such numbers on established plants that they are unmissable. Most effective when planted in drifts or masses where it provides a startling vertical accent. Also effective as an informal hedge or screen. Fresh green growth starts early in the season with initially green flower stems arising from vigorous mounds around midseason with dark purple flowers gradually turning the trademark beige from high summer onwards. Stems are brought to the ground by heavy rainfall, only to spring up again in dry weather. Being virtually sterile, it is a wise choice for large-scale plantings with little risk to surrounding sensitive natural areas. To 1.8 m (6 ft.).

'Overdam'. From the excellent Danish nursery of the same name, this cultivar has bright mounds of green-and-white-striped leaves setting off pinkish feathery plumes of flower. Best colour in cooler climates. To 1.5 m (5 ft.).

Calamagrostis brachytricha

syn *Calamagrostis arundinacea* var. *brachytricha*
KOREAN FEATHER REED GRASS

From mounds of strong green foliage come large upward-pointing arrow-like heads of flowers, initially purple-tinted before quickly fading to a striking buff and beige. Distinctive as an accent in the border or as a drift planting. Generally unfussy about soil type, in its native range it prefers some moisture, whether in sun or the light

Calamagrostis ×acutiflora 'Avalanche'

Calamagrostis ×acutiflora 'Karl Foerster'

shade of the woodland edge. Too much shade or too-dry soil can cause flopping later in the season. Will self-sow under moist conditions to a small extent. From Asia. To 1.2 m (4 ft.). Z4.

Calamagrostis emodensis
CHINESE REED GRASS

With soft-textured bluish green leaves and gently nodding heads of feathery flowers, *C. emodensis* is very pretty if short-lived as a plant. Can slowly spread from its original position. Plant in sunny, well-drained soils for best hardiness. From China. To 1.2 m (4 ft.). Z8.

Calamagrostis epigejos
FEATHER REED GRASS

A variable and strongly spreading species forming thick matts of upright stems topped by usually curving flower spikes. Self-sows readily and is ideal for erosion control or for covering large areas. Will tolerate sun or shade and most soils, though prefers some moisture. From Europe, the U.K. and Asia. To 1.5 m (5 ft.). Z5.

Calamagrostis foliosa
MENDOCINO REED GRASS

Gentle mounds of soft blue-green foliage occasionally streaked purplish red make this geographically limited species quietly attractive, especially when covered with spring-blooming flowers that accentuate the rounded habit on mature specimens. Tolerant of sea spray and winds; a good choice for gardens exposed to coastal conditions. Happy in light shade or full sun with

Calamagrostis brachytricha

enough moisture. Does not respond to being cut back, and will require dividing every few years to maintain vigour. From California. To 45 cm ($1\frac{1}{2}$ ft.). Z8.

Calamagrostis nutkaensis
PACIFIC REED GRASS

Coarse arching green leaves form healthy clumps, from which come upright to slightly pendulous flower stems during spring that persist for some time. Semi-evergreen in mild locations. Found in grasslands, swales and open woodland under moist conditions and will adapt to either shade or sun with enough soil moisture. From the North American Pacific Coast. To 1.2 m (4 ft.). Z7.

Calamagrostis varia
REED GRASS

Slowly spreading roots can make large tussocks of foliage that support upright flower stems and initially deep reddish purple flowers in early summer.

Calamagrostis varia

Found in open woodlands and higher grasslands; in gardens, prefers sun but can tolerate light shade. From Europe. To 1.2 cm (4 ft.). Z5.

Carex
SEDGE

Carex is a genus of mostly evergreen grass-*like* plants: not in fact true grasses, but members of the huge sedge family which includes several thousand species and almost innumerable cultivars. Clump-forming or rapidly running, and capable of adapting to a variety of soil types and climatic conditions as wide as the species are numerous, sedges have become a major part of the gardener's plant palette. Often naturally occurring in moist soils in sun or shade, the ability of many to withstand drought and dry shade is invaluable. Clump-forming types offer foliage in myriad hues with flowers mostly (though not exclusively) of secondary consideration. Running types are especially valuable for tough applications such as erosion control, lawn replacement and green roofs. Widely distributed in temperate areas.

'Silver Sceptre'. Compact and neatly variegated with broad, creamy white margins, the silver sceptre sedge is an excellent garden plant, tolerating wide-ranging conditions from sun to shade and wet to dry. Of uncertain origin in Japan. To 25 cm (10 in.). Z8.

Carex alba
WHITE SEDGE

Gradually spreading, finely textured mounds of bright green foliage make quietly attractive ground cover in conditions from full sun to damp shade. From Europe. To 30 cm (1 ft.). Z5.

Carex albicans

WHITETINGE SEDGE

Tough, low-growing and shade-tolerant, this finely leaved clump-forming semi-evergreen sedge is a sensible choice for woodland areas. From North America. To 20 cm (8 in.). Z4.

Carex arenaria

SAND SEDGE

Found on stabilized sand dunes, this sedge has dark green leaves and is distinctive for the often noticeably straight lines created by its far-reaching running habit. Prefers sunny sandy soils. From Europe and the U.K. To 45 cm (1½ ft.). Z4.

Carex berggrenii

NUTBROWN SEDGE

With low-growing, gradually spreading clumps

Carex 'Silver Sceptre'. Photograph courtesy of Dianna Jazwinski.

of reddish brown leaves. Happy in sun but soil should not be too dry. From New Zealand. To 10 cm (4 in.). Z5.

Carex brunnea

BROWN SEDGE

A widely distributed clump-forming evergreen, usually represented in gardens by shorter-growing variegated cultivars. From Australia and Asia, especially China and Japan. Z8.

'Jenneke'. Tidy mounds of narrow evergreen foliage, brightly striped greenish yellow to cream and green-edged. Best in sun or part shade if not too dry. To 40 cm (16 in.).

'Variegata'. Has similar small mounds of evergreen foliage, but with green-centred creamy white edges. To 40 cm (16 in.).

Carex buchananii

LEATHERLEAF SEDGE

A striking, bright copper-bronze-foliaged plant forming tufted erect mounds with characteristically curled leaf tips. Looks stunning when contrasted well. Drought-tolerant. Comes easily from seed with minor variations, which have given rise to several seed strains such as 'Red Rooster' and 'Viridis'. All can be comparatively short lived. From New Zealand. To 60 cm (2 ft.). Z7.

Carex comans

HAIRY SEDGE

Possibly the most commonly grown brown-foliaged sedge, *C. comans* has given rise to several selections, all differing somewhat in foliage colouration, but broadly forming wider-than-high mounds of evergreen foliage and insignificant flowers. All brown-foliaged sedges can be relatively short lived (lasting three to five years), though timely division can rejuvenate established plants. Will re-seed if happy, allowing for the gradual replacement of older plants. Best in full sun and well-drained soils but will tolerate part shade. From New Zealand. To 45 cm ($1\frac{1}{2}$ ft.). Z7.

'Bronze'. Probably an all-inclusive name for any of the darker forms of the species that come easily from seed.

'Frosted Curls'. A really distinctive form, with pale silvery green foliage curling prettily towards the ground. Best in a sunny, open spot.

'Milk Chocolate'. Has warm chocolate-brown leaves. Of uncertain origin.

Carex conica
HIME-KAN-SUGE

With glossy green leaves forming dense mounds of tufted foliage, *C. conica* is usually only seen in gardens in the variegated form. From Japan and Korea. Z5.

'Snowline' ('Variegata', 'Marginata'). Very attractive, with slowly growing mounds of white-margined deep green leaves which can be relatively long lived. Happy in open sunny positions or light shade if not too dry. To 40 cm (16 in.).

Carex dipsacea

Forms evergreen clumps of dark bronzy olive-green foliage with almost-black flowerheads appearing from within the foliage. Best colour in full sun where not too dry. From New Zealand. To 60 cm (2 ft.). Z7.

'Dark Horse'. Has rather darker, more dramatically coloured foliage in many shades of dark green and olive. Prefers full sun and soil that is not too dry.

Carex divulsa
GREY SEDGE

Beautiful and adaptable, with long dark green leaves forming gracefully drooping mounds of evergreen foliage. Invaluable for garden and wider

use. Dainty if individually unremarkable soft yellow flowers are produced in sufficient numbers to contrast with the foliage's colour and form. Happy in sun or shade and dry to damp soils. From Eurasia and the U.K. To 45 cm ($1\frac{1}{2}$ ft.). Z4.

Carex elata
TUSSOCK SEDGE

Forms dense tussocks of grey-green leaves that slowly make larger stands in wet marginal places such as marshes and riversides. This tough species is not usually seen in gardens other than in its very popular golden-foliaged forms. From Eurasia and the U.K. Z5.

'Aurea'. One of the most striking of all sedges during spring, when its bright golden leaves, variably striped light to dark green, are freely produced—upright at first, then gradually cascading outwards to the ground. The freely produced flowers are most attractive when seen close up, and can add considerably to the overall effect on a mature plant. Best in the early part of the year with enough moisture. Foliage will gradually crisp, especially if dry, though cutting back at this time can stimulate a fresh crop of less bright but still effective leaves. To 75 cm ($2\frac{1}{2}$ ft.).

'Knightshayes'. A less robust form, named for the famous British garden, with leaves of pure gold. To 60 cm (2 ft.).

Carex flacca
CARNATION GRASS, GLAUCOUS SEDGE

The narrow, glaucous, blue, pointed foliage of this gradually spreading sedge resembles that of a garden carnation. Native to sand dunes and marshes, it is tough but attractive—a desirable ornamental, useful as a green roof plant. Occasional dainty purple-black flowers are sometimes numerous enough to be noticeable. Good in sun, drought or light shade. Various selections have been made. From Eurasia, the U.K. and North Africa. To 30 cm (1 ft.). Z4.

'Blue Zinger'. A form with more intense blue to the foliage. Possibly a little taller.

Carex flagellifera
MOP HEAD SEDGE

A brown sedge similar in its generally rounded outline to *C. comans* and *C. testacea*, with a range of foliage colour that has led to several selections including 'Toffee Twist' and 'Coca Cola'. Like other browns, it can be short lived and will seed where happy. Best in full sun and not-too-wet soils. From New Zealand. To 40 cm (16 in.). Z7.

Carex flava
YELLOW SEDGE

Has quietly attractive, subtle light greenish leaves, topped with unusual orange-brown flowers turning to spiky yellow seedheads later in the summer. Occurring naturally in marshes and wet woods, it will also tolerate quite dry conditions. From Eurasia and the U.K. To 60 cm (2 ft.). Z5.

Carex morrowii
syn *Carex fortunei*
KAN SUGE

Easygoing, with gradually spreading mounds of evergreen leaves, it will tolerate a wide range of conditions and is usually seen in gardens as one of the following selected forms. From Japan. Z5.

'Fisher's Form'. Has very attractive, fresh-looking yellow-white and green foliage on compact rosette-forming plants. Equally happy in sun or light shade. To 30 cm (1 ft.).

'Ice Dance'. A spreading form, but makes dense, easily controllable cover with bright green leaves narrowly margined pale creamy white. To 30 cm (1 ft.).

'Silk Tassel'. Technically a cultivar of a markedly different subspecies *C. m.* var. *temnolepis*, this form has very narrow leaves with a refined

Carex elata 'Aurea'

variegation that is white-centred, green-edged and gives an overall impression of grey. Happy in sun or part shade. To 30 cm (1 ft.).

'Variegata'. Encompasses most selections with variegated leaves that have been made over the past century. To 30 cm (1 ft.).

Carex muskingumensis
PALM SEDGE

Slowly increasing, long-lived clumps of architectural, semi-evergreen, narrow light green leaves taper to a point, topped with brown pompom-like flowerheads during summer. From wetter areas, but tolerates quite dry soils in sun or part shade. From North America. To 60 cm (2 ft.). Z4.

'Ice Fountains'. Distinctive, with bright white and dark green leaves.

'Little Midge'. A lovely and genuinely dwarf selection, similar in most respects to the species except smaller in all its parts. Perfectly formed to 15 cm (6 in.).

'Oehme'. Green-foliaged, with amazing narrowly yellow margins gradually appearing as the season progresses.

'Silberstreif'. Slightly more compact, with attractive green-and-white-striped variegated foliage. Best in light shade. To 45 cm (1½ ft.).

Carex nigra
BLACK SEDGE

Found in bogs, waterways and marshy areas, this variable species can be clump forming or running, with foliage in various shades of glaucous green. Flowers are interesting, if unshowy. An excellent ground cover for wet areas, it has given rise to several cultivated forms. From Europe, the U.K. and coastal North America. To 75 cm (2½ ft.). Z5.

'Online'. Forms slowly creeping mounds of grey-green foliage narrowly margined creamy yellow. To 45 cm (1½ ft.).

'Variegata'. Forms slowly spreading mounds of glaucous light-yellow-margined leaves. To 40 cm (16 in.).

Carex obnupta
SLOUGH SEDGE

Makes large clumps of tough, bright green, sharp-edged leaves. Can spread to cover large areas under suitable conditions, such as in wet soils or by the water's edge. Has very attractive purplish black flowers. Best in sun or reasonable shade. From West Coastal U.S. To 1.5 m (5 ft.). Z7.

'Golden Day'. A selection with entirely golden foliage. Less robust than the species. To 1.2 m (4 ft.).

Carex oshimensis
OSHIMA KAN SUGE

A clump-forming, tough and hardy sedge often found in woodland areas in its natural range, and most commonly encountered in gardens in

Carex obnupta 'Golden Day'

variegated forms. From Japan. To 45 cm (1½ ft.). Z5–6.

'Evergold' ('Old Gold', 'Variegata'). Individual leaves are brightly variegated with creamy white to yellow centres and dark green marginal stripes, gradually forming gracefully cascading mounds. Happy in sun or shade in not-too-dry soils. To 40 cm (16 in.).

'Gold Strike'. A variegated selection from Kurt Bluemel, with similar dark green margins and uniformly creamy yellow centres. To 40 cm (16 in.).

Carex panicea
CARNATION SEDGE

Similar to (and often confused with) carnation grass, *C. flacca*, this pretty sedge has blue-green foliage and dainty flowers. Tolerates a wide variety of conditions, from full sun to shade and wet to quite dry soils. From Eurasia and the U.K. To 30 cm (1 ft.). Z7–8.

Carex pansa
CALIFORNIA MEADOW SEDGE

This tough, spreading evergreen sedge is very similar to *C. praegracilis*—very adaptable, and frequently used in meadows and for lawn replacement and restoration projects throughout its widespread range. Happy in sun or some shade, in a wide variety of soil types and in most levels of moisture. From the western U.S. To 40 cm (16 in.). Z6.

Carex pendula
PENDULOUS SEDGE

Makes dense clumps of tough dark green pendulous foliage, from which emerge tall graceful flowering stems with drooping yellow catkin-like flowers. Can re-seed heavily. Tolerates a wide range of conditions, including sun or shade in wet or dry soils. Commonly encountered throughout its range. From Europe, the U.K., Asia and North Africa. To 1.8 m (6 ft.) in flower. Z7.

'Moonraker'. Not often seen, with bright golden yellow young shoots and foliage that gradually returns to the usual green after the spring flush. To 1.5 m (5 ft.).

Carex pensylvanica
PENNSYLVANIA SEDGE

Mostly evergreen, spreading and variable, this widespread species can be found covering large areas with an even, lawn-like sward under trees or in more open conditions. Very drought- and shade-tolerant but will not withstand regular foot traffic. Can be winter-dormant in coldest areas. From eastern North America. To 20 cm (8 in.). Z4.

Carex phyllocephala
CHINESE PALM SEDGE

This unusual species is not often cultivated in gardens, though it is seen in a variegated form. From China. Z7–8.

'Sparkler'. This stunning sedge resembles a star bursting, with its cream, green and white foliage on tall, almost-cane-like stems that are often blotched deep maroon purple. Excellent in a container. Needs adequate moisture and often shelter to do well. To 60 cm (2 ft.).

Carex plantaginea
BROADLEAVED SEDGE

Clump-forming, with distinctive wide, pale green leaves, almost rosette-like. From open woodland in damp areas; can be evergreen, and needs moisture to be happy. From North America. To 40 cm (16 in.). Z5.

Carex praegracilis
WESTERN MEADOW SEDGE
One of the most adaptable sedges. Widespread in its natural range and slowly making its way from West to East Coast in North America, this strongly spreading species makes dense mats of almost-indestructible, usually evergreen foliage that may go summer- or winter-dormant depending on prevailing conditions. From coastal sand dunes to inland meadows, from wet to dry, its tough adaptability makes it a first choice for meadows, lawn replacement and green roofs. When cut on a regular basis it will produce a close sward of foliage that can be kept just a few inches tall. From western North America. To 45 cm (1½ ft.). Z5.

Carex remota
REMOTE SEDGE
Small tussocks of bright green leaves and short, widely spaced pale yellow flower spikes are found in shady, often moist areas and adapt to shade or sun. From Eurasia and the U.K. To 45 cm (1½ ft.). Z6.

Carex riparia
GREATER POND SEDGE
Found in slowly moving or still water and often forming very large drifts over time, this aggressively colonizing pond sedge is usually seen as a variegated form in gardens. Best in sun or light shade. Widespread in the northern hemisphere. To 1.2 m (4 ft.). Z6.

'Variegata'. Gracefully arching leaves are boldly striped white and green. Shares the species' running ability.

Carex secta
NEW ZEALAND TUSSOCK SEDGE
A beautiful evergreen sedge, with nicely coloured clumps of narrow bright green leaves, gradually forming fountains of gently arching foliage that is especially effective near open water. Can eventually form trunks from the old roots and leaf bases, increasing the height of the plant. Prefers sun and adequate moisture but will tolerate some shade if not too dry. From New Zealand. To 1.2 m (4 ft.). Z8.

Carex siderosticha
BROADLEAF SEDGE
Low, dense masses of slowly creeping wide green leaves make excellent durable cover even in dryer woodland conditions, though some sun and moisture are preferred. Has given rise to several mostly variegated forms. Deciduous in winter. From China and Japan. To 20 cm (8 in.). Z5.

'Banana Boat'. Bold and attractive with dramatic yellow-centred variegation. Can lack the other forms' vigour.

'Variegata'. Occasionally pink-tinged, strongly marked white-striped leaves make this the most popular form in gardens. Tolerates relatively dry situations.

Carex solandri
NEW ZEALAND FOREST SEDGE
Broadly similar (but different in detail) to *C. testacea*, with lighter green foliage which assumes a variety of orange to brownish tints that alter with the seasons. Happy in light shade or sun, provided soil is not too dry. From New Zealand. To 60 cm (2 ft.). Z7.

Carex spissa
SAN DIEGO SEDGE
A sedge with attitude. Large steely blue-grey, wide, toothed leaves with noticeable midribs are produced in stout clumps in sun or shady areas where there is sufficient moisture. Light brown flowers are freely produced in spring. Non-

invasive and drought-tolerant once established. From California and Mexico. To 1.5 m (5 ft.). Z7.

Carex stricta
TUSSOCK SEDGE
Forms dense tussocks of bright green foliage, often connected by underground runners that can make large stands in wetlands, marshes and wet woods. Freely produces yellow-brown arching flower stems. Can tolerate drier conditions. From the northeastern U.S. To 90 cm (3 ft.). Z4.

Carex tenuiculmis
BROWN SEDGE
A graceful semi-arching open habit and distinctive chocolate-coloured foliage make this a useful addition to the brown range of sedges. Prefers sun or light shade and not-too-dry soils. From New Zealand. To 60 cm (2 ft.). Z6.

'Cappuccino'. Selected for its attractive, warm, milky-coffee-coloured foliage.

Carex testacea
ORANGE SEDGE
Deservedly one of the most popular sedges, forming striking loose clumps of attractive orange-green foliage that changes subtly throughout the seasons. The arching habit is even more pronounced in tall containers, where the tightly rounded dark seedheads can hang well clear of even the extended evergreen foliage. Best colour in full sun. From New Zealand. To 60 cm (2 ft.). Z6.

'Old Gold'. Has more old gold colouration to its foliage.

Carex trifida
NEW ZEALAND BLUE SEDGE
One of the bigger sedges, with large keeled green leaves with glaucous undersides, most noticeable in sun. Unusual chunky flowerheads of light

Carex tenuiculmis 'Cappuccino'

Carex trifida. Photograph courtesy of Dianna Jazwinski.

brown are especially striking in the early season. Prefers sun or light shade. Drought-tolerant, but dislikes cold areas. From New Zealand. To 90 cm (3 ft.). Z8.

'Rekohu Sunrise'. Striking, with attractive warm yellow, gold and grey-green variegated foliage. To 75 cm ($2\frac{1}{2}$ ft.).

Chasmanthium
WILD OAT

Growing happily in shady conditions, the warm-season deciduous perennial upright grasses that make up this small group are especially useful in gardens. Originally part of the genus *Uniola*.

Chasmanthium latifolium
WILD OAT SPANGLE GRASS

With wide, ribbon-like, bright green leaves on perky upright stems, this grass is happy in relatively dry shady conditions, though stems may be a little more lax than in more open conditions where foliage is a lighter green. Almost-flat spikes of nodding flowers are highly attractive and turn a procession of green to gold and browns, as does foliage as autumn approaches. Clump-forming and tolerant of clay soils and drought, it is versatile for use in many garden applications. Self-seeds in wetter conditions. From North America. To 1.2 m (4 ft.). Z5.

'River Mist'. Has strongly creamy white variegated leaves, and perhaps a slightly more compact habit than the species. Happy in part shade. Seedlings will revert to green. To 90 cm (3 ft.).

Chasmanthium laxum
SLENDER WILD OAT

Clump-forming and taller than wild oat, with smaller flower spikes held clear of the leaves. Happy in light shade and not-too-dry soils. From North America. To 1.5 m (5 ft.). Z6.

Chionochloa
This small group of tussock-forming cool-season evergreen grasses is closely related to *Cortaderia*. Covering large areas of grassland in their native Australasia, they are seldom planted in significant number in gardens.

Chionochloa conspicua
PLUMED TUSSOCK GRASS

Often found near streamsides and other wet places, producing large, open, airy flower stems from relatively coarse and rough foliage. Prefers sun. From New Zealand. To 2.1 m (7 ft.). Z8.

Chionochloa flavicans
TUSSOCK GRASS

More common in gardens than *C. conspicua*, with tough evergreen foliage. Very long-lived and drought-tolerant. Distinctive light greenish yellow flowerheads are attractive when grown well. Happy in sun or light shade and not-too-dry soils. From New Zealand. To 90 cm (3 ft.). Z8.

Chionochloa rubra
RED TUSSOCK GRASS

Grown for its wonderful warm, brassy brown to golden evergreen leaves that form mounds of gently arching foliage that moves in the slightest breeze. Happy in sun and drought-tolerant once established. From New Zealand. To 1.2 m (4 ft.). Z8.

Cortaderia
This group of warm-season evergreens includes the popular, and sometimes overused, pampas grass, as well as more than twenty different species that can offer flowers of amazingly airy gracefulness. All have tough and relatively coarse semi-evergreen leaves and make substantial clumps with age. Although tolerant of a wide range of garden conditions, nearly all perform best in

Chionochloa rubra

In October, the trial border at the RHS Garden Wisley showcases the
wide variety of shapes and forms that pampas have to offer.

sunny, open positions. While the pampas' popularity has often led to inappropriate use, there is little doubting the blowsy magnificence of the individual flowers or the breathtaking effect of a well-grown plant in full bloom.

Cortaderia fulvida
syn *Cortaderia conspicua*
TUSSOCK GRASS
Often confused with *C. richardii* in gardens, this species is seldom seen. Blooms in midsummer, with delicate nodding heads of flower topping mounds of green leaves that are noticeably larger than those of *C. richardii*. Prefers some moisture and open conditions. From New Zealand. To 2.1 m (7 ft.). Z8.

Cortaderia jubata
PURPLE PAMPAS GRASS
A large and vigorous grass. Well-adapted to drier conditions, it has become an invasive weed in sensitive areas where it had been introduced as a cultivated plant. Large mounds of tough leaves and tall, thick stems support often-huge, fluffy flowers in all shades of pink and rose eventually fading to tan. Will re-seed in warm climates. Prefers sun or light shade. From South America. To 2.7 m (9 ft.). Z8.

'Candy Floss'. An English seed-raised selection with large heads of flower in a particularly good shade of pink. Prefers sun.

Cortaderia richardii
TOETOE
Possibly the most graceful of all cortaderias, with relatively early, freely produced nodding brown to tan and beige flowers and gently pendulous long stems that fan outwards to create tall, airy fountains that are distinctive and beautiful. Leaves can be pale grey-green with distinct midribs, and

form quite significant mounds over time. Versatile in its tolerance of wet to fairly dry soils and full sun or semi-shade. From New Zealand. To 2.7 m (9 ft.). Z8.

Cortaderia selloana
syn *Cortaderia argentea*
PAMPAS GRASS
A major constituent of the iconic South American grasslands (the pampas that inspired its common name). Most gardeners are only too familiar with the ability of its tough, sharp-edged leaves to cut skin. In late summer, stiff, robust, upright flower stems produce the often-huge feather-duster-like blooms that have made this grass such a widely used (and frequently misused) plant. Drought-tolerant and very adaptable, an ability to set copious seed makes it a serious weed in warm areas but

Cortaderia selloana 'Evita'

poses no such problem in colder climates, where it is still a treasured garden plant and continues to give rise to cultivars—many compact or with variegated foliage, and frequently both. Most forms are happy in full sun to part shade and most soil types. From South America. Z6–8.

'Alboineata' ('Silver Stripe'). An old cultivar, with bright white-striped leaves. To 2.1 m (7 ft.).

'Aureolineata' ('Gold Band'). With possibly the brightest deep yellow golden and green stripes. Of modest size, though occasional specimens can make large mounds. To 1.8 m (6 ft.).

'Evita'. A recent selection, chiefly of interest for its very compact free-flowering habit. Mounds of typical green foliage are topped by very short-stemmed, large, fluffy white flowers from high summer onwards. To 1.8 m (6 ft.).

'Monstrosa'. Of all *C. s.* forms, produces the largest flowers on the tallest stems. Not for very small gardens. To 3 m (10 ft.) or taller.

'Patagonia'. A first-class introduction, with blue-grey leaves and pinkish plumes on compact plants. Noticeably resistant to cold temperatures. To 2.1 m (7 ft.).

'Point du Raz' (also known as. *C.* 'Point du Raz'). With mid-green leaves edged creamy white and consequently a little slower in growth. Fairly free-flowering. To 1.8 m (6 ft.).

'Pumila'. Arguably one of the best-performing selected forms of pampas, and certainly one of the hardiest, with many handsome heads of freely produced typical flowers in late summer. Good grey-green foliage. To 2.4 m (8 ft.).

'Rendatleri'. The best-known purplish pink-flowered form of *C. s.* To 2.7 m (9 ft.).

'Silver Comet'. With a white-striped variegated that is brighter, and perhaps better, than that of 'Alboineata'. To 2.4 m (8 ft.).

'Splendid Star'. A recently introduced dwarf pampas with gold-streaked green leaves topped with white flower plumes in late summer. To 1.5 m (5 ft.).

'Sunningdale Silver'. The best-known selection among larger pampas. Can make massive fountain-like mounds of grey-green foliage from which arise numerous tall stately flower spikes at about 3 m (10 ft.).

Cortaderia toetoe
TOETOE

Only recently discovered on New Zealand's North Island. Very similar to *C. richardii*, with which it shares many characteristics as well as its common name. To 2.7 m (9 ft.). Z8.

Cyperus
UMBRELLA SEDGE

Comprising hundreds of species widely distributed in temperate and tropical areas worldwide, this mostly evergreen group is second only to *Carex* as the most numerous in the family of sedges. From refined elegance to aggressive weed, umbrella sedges come in many shapes and sizes, though all prefer moisture and are happiest in full sun or light shade. As with any large and complex group of plants there is some confusion about accurate naming, and many of the more tropical species can be used as indoor plants.

Cyperus involucratus
syn *Cyperus alternifolius*
UMBRELLA PLANT

Easy to grow, and happy in full sun or light shade and moist soils to marginal conditions. Commonly found as a water garden specimen or as a house plant in colder areas. Shiny upright stems are topped with wide umbrella-like green bracts which support tiny yellowish flowers—a handsome feature. From Africa. To 90 cm (3 ft.). Z8.

Cyperus longus

GALINGALE

Found in coastal marshes and wet areas, this attractive species has green stems supporting distinctive long-leaved 'umbrellas' which can make very architectural if spreading mounds in wet, sunny areas. From Asia, North Africa, Eurasia and the U.K. To 1.2 m (4 ft.). Z7.

Cyperus papyrus

EGYPTIAN PAPER REED, PAPYRUS

The source of original papyrus writing paper—and probably the most elegant and refined *Cyperus* species, with huge domed heads of narrow, threadlike green growths radiating from a central point. Mature specimens are studded with myriad tiny yellow flowers. Happy in warm areas, in open water or on the edge of a pond, and can make large, gently spreading clumps of tall evergreen stems. In colder areas it is often used as a specimen in ponds or containers in summer and overwintered at about 10°C (50°F). Native to the Nile River Delta. To 4.5 m (15 ft.). Z9.

Deschampsia

HAIR GRASS

This widely distributed group of clump-forming cool-season evergreen grasses includes some invaluable gardenworthy plants. Found in a variety of conditions from meadows to woodland and in wet to dry soils, all have freely produced, delicate-looking flowers that can obscure the foliage.

Deschampsia cespitosa

TUFTED HAIR GRASS

Preferring moist open areas from boggy meadows to edges of woodland, this adaptable grass forms usually-dark-green mounds of leaves that are completely obscured by billowing masses of cloudlike flowers, initially greenish yellow before gradually fading to a fine lace-like beige that stands virtually intact all winter. Excellent at the front of borders as a foil for other, more solid plants, or as informal hedges, and quite superb in drifts and for open grassland effects. Lives longest with some moisture and sun; may be rejuvenated by occasional dividing. Comes easily from seed—partially explaining why some established cultivars have become mixed in the trade. Seed-raised strains continue to be developed for use as low-resource-use turf grass. From temperate U.S., Asia, Eurasia and the U.K. To 1.2 m (4 ft.). Z6.

'Bronzeschleier'. Chosen for its fresh-looking flowers, greenish bronze upon opening. To 90 cm (3 ft.).

'Goldtau'. A highly regarded, relatively compact form with possibly finer-textured flowers. To 90 cm (3 ft.).

Deschampsia cespitosa 'Goldtau'

'Northern Lights'. With compact mounds of occasionally pink-suffused leaves prettily striped creamy white and green. Can be comparatively short lived. To 45 cm (1½ ft.).

'Schottland'. Robust, dark green clumps of foliage support relatively tall, sturdy flowers. An excellent selection, made in Scotland.

var. *vivipara* ('Fairy's Joke'). Uncommon but distinctive, producing live young plants on the flowers' ends, which are weighted down in consequence. To 75 cm (2½ ft.).

Deschampsia cespitosa subsp. *holciformis*
PACIFIC HAIR GRASS

Often found on coastal bluffs or in open grasslands. Much more compact in all its parts than the species. Low-growing, with distinctive, more densely packed spikes of flower. For a range of soils; prefers sun. From the western U.S. To 40 cm (16 in.). Z7.

Deschampsia flexuosa
HAIR GRASS

A finer-textured and more drought-tolerant version of tufted hair grass, happier in drier situations including relatively dry shade. It is also more compact, though less often seen in gardens than its more robust cousin. Will seed where happy. From temperate North America, Eurasia and the U.K. To 60 cm (2 ft.). Z6.

'Aurea' ('Hohe Tatra', 'Tatra Gold'). Foliage on low-growing plants is golden yellow, with best colour in cooler areas. Can be weak and short-lived if not happy. Will come reasonably true from seed. To 40 cm (16 in.).

Desmoschoenus
SAND SEDGE

This genus comprises just one species—an evergreen grass-like sedge from New Zealand.

Desmoschoenus spiralis
GOLDEN SAND SEDGE

This New Zealand version of marram or dune grass has suffered a decline due to being outcompeted by the introduced European species. Tough yellow-green leaves arise from questing fibrous root systems that survive and help to stabilize coastal sand dunes throughout its native habitat, where restoration schemes are helping this species to make a comeback. From New Zealand. To 90 cm (3 ft.). Z8.

Distichlis
SALT GRASS

This small group of tough warm-season semi-evergreen grasses tolerates many coastal situations, mostly in North and South America but also in Australasia.

Distichlis spicata
SALT GRASS

Tough and adaptable, salt grass copes with a variety of coastal as well as inland conditions from dry to distinctly moist, where its creeping habit allows it to make dense ground-hugging mats of spiky foliage. Useful for erosion control, in bioswales, and as a lawn replacement that will tolerate light foot traffic. Prefers open conditions. From North and South America. To 45 cm (1½ ft.). Z4–7.

Elymus

WILD RYE, WHEATGRASS

Grown in gardens primarily for their attractive foliage ranging from soft, glaucous grey-green to strong, steely blue, this large group of mostly cool-season, largely perennial grasses can be either clumping or spreading. Found in a wide variety of mostly open habitats including coastal dunes, prairies and meadow; some may even be found in light woodland. The common name of wheatgrass refers to the flowerheads which are characteristically spiky and open with a strong resemblance to well-known cereal crops. Widely distributed in temperate areas.

Elymus canadensis

CANADA WILD RYE

Found widely throughout much of North America where it is happy in conditions ranging from moist streamsides to dry sandy soils. Relatively short-lived but fast-growing, this clump-former has rather coarse foliage ranging from glaucous green, topped with nodding rye-like flowers. Its ability to seed makes it well-placed for meadow or restoration work, but perhaps less so for garden situations. From North America. To 1.8 m (6 ft.). Z3.

Elymus elymoides

SQUIRREL TAIL

Adapted to a wide variety of different soil types from dry mountain to desert and grassland, always preferring sunny open positions. Its common name refers to the tight hordeum-like flowers that are often noticeably pinkish red. From North America, including Mexico. To 45 cm (1½ ft.). Z6–8.

Elymus hystrix

BOTTLEBRUSH GRASS

One of few true grasses that will happily tolerate reasonable levels of dry shade, though also happy in sun and even moist soils. From clumps of relatively coarse greenish foliage and stiff stems come very showy upright-pointing bottlebrush-like flowers in summer. Known by many gardeners by its synonym *Hystrix patula*, it has recently been transferred to *Elymus* as its ability to hybridize with other members of this group suggests a strong family tie. From North America. To 90 cm (3 ft.). Z3.

Elymus magellanicus

syn *Agropyron magellanicum*

BLUE WHEATGRASS

Valued for its intense silvery blue clumps of slowly spreading semi-evergreen leaves that secure its reputation as one of the bluest of grasses. Dislikes high, humid night temperatures and requires sunny, well-drained soils. From South America. To 60 cm (2 ft.). Z6.

RECLASSIFICATION OF *ELYMUS* SPECIES

Elymus is closely related to *Leymus*, to which several species have recently been reclassified:

Elymus arenarius is now *Leymus arenarius* (page 211), *E. cinereus* now *L. cinereus* (page 212), *E. condensatus* now *L. condensatus* (page 212), *E. mollis* now *L. mollis* (page 212) and *E. racemosus* now *L. racemosus* (page 212).

Elymus solandri

syn *Triticum solandri*

WHEATGRASS

Rather wider than high, and with a slowly spreading habit, this interesting wheatgrass often has very blue foliage which is always at its best in full sun. Coming from well-drained but not too dry coastal rocky sites to higher mountain elevations, it is happy in similar garden situations and excellent in containers where it can develop its trailing habit. From New Zealand.To 45 cm (1½ ft.). Z7.

Eragrostis

LOVEGRASS

This very large group of more than three hundred annual and perennial species, often-warm-season deciduous grasses, are found in a variety of (usually) sunny areas worldwide. Those most commonly used in gardens are perennials that will seed under suitable conditions. Widely distributed in temperate to tropical areas.

Eragrostis chloromelas

syn *Eragrostis curvula* var. *conferta*

BOER LOVEGRASS

Although now classified by many botanists under the variable species *E. curvula*, this form is clearly identifiable in gardens by its attractive silvery glaucous blue foliage and by being noticeably less cold-tolerant than *E. curvula*. Happy in a reasonable range of soils, and drought-tolerant though always best in sun. Masses of delicately airy flowers give a gently cascading effect when in full bloom. Comes true from seed, so may be considered a strain. From Africa and Asia. To 90 cm (3 ft.). Z7.

Eragrostis curvula

AFRICAN LOVEGRASS

A graceful species. Long used not just for ornamental purposes but also for stabilization and even forage, it has been widely introduced to different areas for those purposes. Well-behaved in cooler climates where it has proved more tough and hardy than its South African origin might suggest, it can seed aggressively, becoming a weed in warmer areas. Rounded tussocks of fine hair-like bright green leaves, highly ornamental in themselves, support many finely arching flower stems and delicate, airy flowerheads that can cover the foliage in a haze of light green fading to tan and beige. Useful in many gardens situations, always preferring sun. From South Africa but widely naturalized. To 1.2 m (4 ft.). Z6.

'S&SH10'. A selection that has yet to receive its own name. Has distinctly larger heads of

Elymus hystrix. Photograph courtesy of Dianna Jazwinski.

Eragrostis curvula 'Totnes Burgundy'

flower and is among the tallest forms of the species. To 1.5 m (5 ft.).

'Totnes Burgundy'. A wonderful selection found by Julian and Sarah Sutton, with mature leaves turning a stunning deep burgundy red from the tips down and long arching sprays of insignificant beige flowers. Seedlings will revert to the straight species. Excels in containers where its gradually pendulous foliage habit can be best appreciated. To 90 cm (3 ft.).

Eragrostis elliottii
LOVEGRASS

Not often seen in cultivation, the true species is found in coastal pine and oak woodland. Has relatively bluish green leaves and compact spikes of flower. Many of the plants in cultivation,

Eragrostis curvula

especially in the United States, are likely to be forms of *E. chloromelas* which itself is now regarded as a form of *E. curvula*. From North and South America. To 75 cm (2½ ft.). Z8.

'Tallahassee Sunset'. A selection from John Greenlee, with particularly glaucous blue leaves.

Eragrostis spectabilis
PURPLE LOVEGRASS

Named for its spectacular clouds of pinkish purple flowers, freely produced on relatively compact clumps of basal foliage when happy. Can be short lived but will re-seed. Always happiest in sun; may be disappointing in mild, maritime areas with lower light levels. Widely distributed on sandy soils. From North and South America. To 60 cm (2 ft.). Z5.

Eragrostis trichodes
SAND LOVEGRASS

Of similar height to African lovegrass and coming from sandy open areas, sand lovegrass is attractive, easy growing and very drought tolerant. Produces masses of spectacular shimmering reddish pink panicles that can cover the basal clumps of green foliage. From the U.S. To 1.2 m (4 ft.). Z5.

'Bend'. With less robust stems that bend under the weight of freely produced flowers. To 90 cm (3 ft.).

Eriophorum
COTTON GRASS

The common name for this family of grass-like sedges refers to the cotton-like woolly, often

Eragrostis spectabilis

white but occasionally tan flowers that all species produce profusely. Clump-forming or spreading, all twenty or so species prefer the cooler conditions of wet, boggy, acidic soils mostly open to full sun. Individually beautiful and quite spectacular en masse. Occurs mostly in the northern hemisphere.

Eriophorum angustifolium

COMMON COTTON GRASS, COTTON SEDGE
Simply breathtaking in autumn when the white flowers, which are actually more bristle-like than cottony, are in full bloom. Long running roots can over time form large masses of narrow grass-like leaves that cover open boggy areas. From Eurasia, the U.K., Greenland and North America. To 60 cm (2 ft.). Z3.

Eriophorum latifolium

BROADLEAVED COTTON GRASS
Wider-leaved than its more commonly encountered cousin *E. angustifolium*, and often occurring on richer soils. Slowly spreading, with the usual white cotton heads of flower. From Eurasia and the U.K. To 60 cm (2 ft.). Z4.

Eriophorum vaginatum

HARE'S TAIL
Distinguished by single flower spikes. Slowly spreading, with densely tufted clumps. Common in peaty moorlands. From Eurasia, the U.K. and North America. To 60 cm (2 ft.). Z4.

Eriophorum virginicum

TAWNY COTTON GRASS, VIRGINIA COTTON GRASS
Distinctive for its often-tan-coloured cotton flowers produced from long spreading roots. Widespread and common throughout its range in moist meadows, bogs and other wet areas. From North America. To 90 cm (3 ft.). Z3.

Festuca

FESCUE
A huge group of characteristically perennial, fine-foliaged evergreen grasses coming from sunny open areas ranging from mountains to meadows. Being cool-season, they are not adapted to hot humid climates. Garden forms are mostly clump forming, though some are spreading including those used as turfgrass and in traditional lawns. Relatively short-lived as a group, regular division will maintain youth and vigour while most species can be easily raised from seed. All prefer sun and some soil moisture in drier climates. Widely distributed in temperate areas.

Festuca amethystina

TUFTED FESCUE
Tidy rounded clumps of finely rolled, usually mid to dark green leaves support gently pendulous flower stems that can vary in shades of pinky red. Initially violet-tinted to purple flowers are particularly effective in early parts of the year. Variable

Eriophorum virginicum

from seed, which has given rise to several selections. From Central Europe. To 60 cm (2 ft.). Z4.

'Superba'. A long-established selection, with especially blue-grey leaves and striking pinky purple flower stems. Seed-raised plants will vary in stem and leaf colour.

Festuca californica
CALIFORNIA FESCUE

Frequently dormant during the dry season; the onset of autumn rain sees new silvery blue-green stiffly arching leaves appear from the resting mounds, to be followed by delicate airy blue-grey spikes of flower that fade beige. Drought-tolerant

Festuca amethystina. Photograph courtesy of Dianna Jazwinski.

and happy even in light shade in high-sunlight areas. Has given rise to several notable cultivars. From the western U.S. To 90 cm (3 ft.). Z7.

'Horse Mountain Green'. Noteworthy for its rather taller flower spikes that can reach up to 1.5 m (5 ft.) in favoured places.

Festuca glauca
BLUE FESCUE

This species has given rise to various commonly seen, tufted, mound-shaped cultivars and forms valued for their fine, narrow leaves in myriad shades of grey and silver to blue. With their propensity for setting viable seed, the older cultivars' original material has likely been adulterated so that some are now simply regarded as seed-raised strains, many of which have some garden merit. Most will produce upright flower stems, initially blue-grey but quickly drying a strawy beige. Where foliage colour is of primary interest, a regular pruning or shearing of old growth in spring will often prevent flowering and maintain foliage quality. From southern France. To 40 cm (16 in.). Z4.

'Blue Fox'. An old variety, with steely blue foliage.

'Blue Note'. With excellent blue coloration and good tolerance to drier and warmer conditions.

'Boulder Blue'. Well-adapted to steppe-like conditions, with steely blue-grey foliage.

'Elijah Blue'. In its true form, still regarded as one of the bluest and best-growing selections—the standard by which others are judged.

'Golden Toupee'. Currently the only yellow-foliaged form, with attractive warm yellow foliage and flower stems. Very short-lived if not happy.

'Siskiyou Blue' (also known as *F.* 'Siskiyou Blue'). A wonderful selection, originally thought to be *F. idahoensis*, with very silvery blue, relatively long leaves making quite superb drooping mounds if not cut back.

Festuca idahoensis

IDAHO FESCUE

One of the most widely distributed and common fescues within its range, preferring mostly open dry habitats from sea level to mountain meadow. Variable from seed but generally forming tight clumps of silvery blue-grey leaves and flower stems, eventually fading to straw, sometimes flushed pink. From western North America. To 60 cm (2 ft.). Z4.

'Snow Mountain'. Blue-grey leaves and slightly larger size distinguish this Nevin Smith selection.

'Tomales Bay'. A wonderful blue-grey-leaved selection, forming relatively compact mounds of strong, healthy foliage.

Festuca mairei

ATLAS FESCUE

Slower-growing and longer-lived than most other fescues, forming relatively large mounds of rather tough grey-green leaves. Individually somewhat indistinguishable, en masse the narrow flower stems add considerably to the charm of this much-underused species. Best planted sufficiently far apart to appreciate the plants' distinct rounded outline. Prefers sunny open positions and dislikes winter wet soils. From Morocco. To 75 cm ($2\frac{1}{2}$ ft.). Z5.

Festuca glauca

Festuca ovina

SHEEP'S FESCUE

Common on poor moorland and upland soils where it can become a popular fodder crop, this species has limited ornamental value. Many of the blue garden fescues ascribed by various authorities (and often-incorrect nursery catalogues) to *Festuca ovina* in fact belong to the wide-ranging *Festuca glauca*. From Eurasia and the U.K. To 60 cm (2 ft.). Z5.

Festuca rubra

RED FESCUE

Often used as lawn or turf grass, with many seed-raised strains identified explicitly for this purpose. As a lawn substitute, un-mown or even infrequently mown, it can produce loose meadow-like swards of fine hair-like foliage that will accept some foot traffic. Widely distributed and ubiquitous throughout its range, it comes easily from seed and has provided numerous regionally adapted cultivars for garden and green roof use. Slowly spreading clumps tolerate wide-ranging soil conditions including drought. Prefers sun but will tolerate light shade. From Eurasia, the U.K. and North America. To 30 cm (1 ft.). Z4.

'Jughandle'. A Californian coastal selection with compact dense blue-grey foliage.

'Molate Blue'. A drought-tolerant selection with grey-green leaves.

'Patrick's Point'. Ideal for green roof and lawn use, with fine grey-green leaves in slowly spreading tight clumps.

Festuca valesiaca

WALLIS FESCUE

Similar in most respects to blue fescues, this species and its better-known form is typically more compact than *Festuca glauca* types. From Eurasia. To 15 cm (6 in.). Z5.

var. *glaucantha*. With blue-green foliage on 15-cm (6-in.) high mounds.

Glyceria

MANNA, SWEET GRASS, SWEET REED GRASS

These warm-season evergreen grasses are found in wet places such as marshes and on the edges of open water. The common name of sweet grass refers to the tasty seeds and foliage that waterfowl and livestock respectively find to their liking. Widely distributed in temperate areas.

Glyceria grandis

AMERICAN MANNA GRASS

Can form extensive masses of mid green leaves and summer-blooming upright flowers. Native to

Festuca ovina

marshes, rivers and swampy areas, it prefers permanently damp to moist conditions and open sun. Widely distributed in North America. To 1.5 m (5 ft.). Z3.

Glyceria maxima
MANNA GRASS

Aggressively spreading roots help to stablish large patches of green foliage that support tall, graceful panicles of flower in shallow water such as ponds or lakes. Will establish in almost any soil provided there is sufficient moisture. Prefers sunny open positions but will accept some light shade. From Asia and Eurasia. To 2.1 m (7 ft.). Z6.

var. *variegata*. More commonly seen in gardens than the species, with bright creamy-white-striped leaves that can be pink-tinged in

cooler conditions. Flowers rarely and is less vigorous than the green form, but still very much a spreader. Ideal for planting banks and for the water's edge. To 60 cm (2 ft.).

Hakonechloa
HAKONE GRASS

Containing only one species, this beautiful and versatile warm-season deciduous grass comes from relatively moist conditions in the mountains of Japan.

Hakonechloa macra
HAKONE GRASS

Spreads so slowly that it can practically be regarded as clump-forming. Very long-lived, tough and durable, it will gradually make

Glyceria maxima var. *variegata*

dense weed-proof cover in a variety of garden conditions from full sun to quite dark shade provided the soil has sufficient moisture. Generally unfussy about soil, though slower in heavy clays. Often used around tree bases, where its shiny lanceolate pointed leaves make an attractive even-textured outline that ripples most effectively in the slightest breeze. Grown for its foliage effect; flowers are dainty and light, and can go almost unnoticed among the leaves. Has given rise to several, mostly Japanese, cultivars. Less happy in hot and humid climates. To 75 cm ($2\frac{1}{2}$ ft.). Z3–6.

'Albovariegata' ('Albostriata'). Irregular bright white, cream and light green striped leaves make for a striking, slowly increasing mound of pointed foliage that is happy in sun or part shade where its refined colouration can lighten an otherwise dull corner. Possibly more heat-tolerant than the golden-variegated forms.

'All Gold'. A recent selection with, as its name suggests, bright yellow-gold leaves without any trace of green. Slowly spreading mounds are happiest in some shade, at least in warmer climates. To 60 cm (2 ft.).

'Aureola' ('Alboaurea'). Forms strong, slowly spreading mounds of gold-and-green-striped foliage that takes on an almost chartreuse-green colouration in shade and turns a much brighter brassy yellow in sun. Probably the most commonly seen *H. m.* cultivar, with multiple garden uses from durable and attractive cover around tree bases to ground cover in open sun. Like all hakone grasses, excellent in pots and containers where the foliage's cascading effect can be appreciated. To 45 cm ($1\frac{1}{2}$ ft.).

'Beni Fuchi'. A compact, slow-growing form with bronzed leaves that turn shades of red with autumn's cooler temperatures. Uncommon outside of its homeland. To 30 cm (1 ft.).

'Mulled Wine' ('Luccarred'). A compact

selection from *H. m.* 'Aureola', with very similar golden-striped leaves that can have striking burgundy red colouration, especially on new foliage, growing more pronounced as the season progresses. To 45 cm ($1\frac{1}{2}$ ft.).

'Nicolas'. Slightly more compact than the species, with an attractive wine red colouration on bright green leaves. To 45 cm ($1\frac{1}{2}$ ft.).

'Stripe It Rich'. A recent selection from 'All Gold', with a white central stripe on otherwise lightly golden foliage. To 45 cm ($1\frac{1}{2}$ ft.).

Helictotrichon

OAT GRASS

Clump-forming and semi-evergreen, this group of cool-season grasses comprises more than one hundred perennial species, most commonly represented in gardens by the blue oat.

Hakonechloa macra 'Aureola'

Helictotrichon sempervirens

BLUE OAT GRASS

Comes from often dry, rocky mountain areas where it forms attractive silky-looking mounds of metallic blue spiky-ended leaves. Happiest in dry, open, sunny positions but will accept some shade in higher-sunlight areas. Excellent as specimens in gravel gardens or other dry plantings, especially where the plants' gently pendulous flower stems can add greatly to their overall effect. Also highly effective in meadows as a drift, though ideally there should be sufficient space between plants for the individually mounding habit to be appreciated. In warm or damp climates it can suffer from rust, in which case affected foliage should be cut back. From Eurasia. To 90 cm (3 ft.). Z4.

'Pendulum'. A seldom-seen selection with strongly pendulous flowers that are possibly more freely produced than the species'. To 75 cm (2½ ft.).

Helictotrichon sempervirens

'Saphirsprudel'. With bright silvery blue leaves that are supposedly more rust resistant.

Holcus

VELVET GRASS

This small group of perennial clump-forming or spreading cool-season deciduous grasses has widely naturalized. Found in open grasslands or by open woodland edge. From temperate Africa, North America, the U.K. and Eurasia. Z5–6.

Holcus lanatus

VELVET GRASS, YORKSHIRE FOG

Usually peaking early in the season, this clump-former's leaves are soft, velvety and often coloured a distinctive grey-green. Upright stems hold soft-textured flowers in myriad shades of pink through white. Best in open sunny spots but will tolerate some light shade. From Asia, Eurasia and North America. To 90 cm (3 ft.). Z5.

Holcus mollis

CREEPING SOFT GRASS

Considered a weedy species that will self sow-in most situations; more often seen in its variegated form. From Asia, Eurasia and North America. To 90 cm (3 ft.). Z5.

'Variegatus' ('Albovariegatus'). The most commonly grown form, though dwindling in popularity. Chosen for its creeping but more compact habit and often heavily white-striped leaves. Several slightly differing forms are grown under this name. Prefers sun or light shade in a variety of soils. To 30 cm (1 ft.).

Hordeum

FOXTAIL BARLEY

This group of annual and perennial cool-season deciduous grasses includes the common barley, *Hordeum vulgare*. All species share the signature squirrel-tail-like barley flowers that have given rise to so many descriptive common names. Widely distributed in temperate regions.

Hordeum jubatum

FOX SQUIRRELTAIL, WILD BARLEY

Widely naturalized and common in gardens in many parts of the world. Clumps of slight foliage produce highly distinctive reddish pink angular flowers strongly resembling cultivated barley, at their brightest when first open. Happy in dry soils in sun. Can produce flowers over a long period, especially if cut back at any point during the growing season. Relatively short-lived, plants come easily from seed. From North America. To 75 cm ($2\frac{1}{2}$ ft.). Z5.

Imperata

SATIN TAIL, BLOOD GRASS

These strongly spreading perennial warm-season deciduous grasses can be invasive weeds in warmer climates. Widely distributed in temperate and tropical regions.

Imperata brevifolia

SATIN TAIL

Found only in moist meadows and named for its attractive, fluffy, satiny white flowerheads produced from gradually spreading mounds of bright green foliage. Prefers moist soils in sun. From the southern U.S. To 1.2 m (4 ft.). Z7.

Imperata cylindrica

An exceptionally variable species that appears to contain both aggressive and unaggressive strains, thought to originate from tropical and temperate areas respectively. Banned in many warmer areas, where its spreading tendencies and ability to seed identify it as a noxious weed. From China, Korea and Japan. To 90 cm (3 ft.). Z6.

Holcus lanatus

Hordeum jubatum. Photograph courtesy of Dianna Jazwinski.

'Rubra' ('Red Baron'). Selected for its stunning deep red colouration that starts mostly at the leaf tips and works it way down the leaf as the season ages. Although a perfect garden plant, slowly spreading and non-flowering in temperate areas, there is still a risk of the parent species' invasiveness showing though in warmer climates. Can be very slow to establish, especially on some colder, heavier soils. Often grown in containers where it makes a strong impact. Best colour in sun. To 30 cm (1 ft.).

Imperata cylindrica 'Rubra'. Photograph courtesy of Dianna Jazwinski.

Jarava

syn *Stipa*

FEATHER GRASS, NEEDLE GRASS

These mostly perennial, cool-season, evergreen clump-forming grasses are related to *Nassella* and remain included in the larger genus of *Stipa* according to some botanical authorities.

Jarava ichu

syn *Stipa ichu*

Clumps of soft, light green hair-like leaves form healthy clumps of quick-growing foliage bearing a strong likeness to that of the closely related and deservedly popular pony tail grass *Nassella tenuissima* (syn *Stipa tenuissima*). The resemblance ends with this species' long, narrow, fluffy white flowers that form spectacular airy clumps, waving dramatically and seductively in the slightest wind. Very drought-tolerant. Requires well-drained soils, or a well-placed container, in plenty of sun. From South America. To 90 cm (3 ft.). Z8.

Juncus

RUSH

This huge group comprises more than two hundred species of mostly perennial evergreen grass-like rushes, distinguishable by their unique narrow, rounded, strongly vertical stems that lack leaves but carry generally insignificant flowerheads either on top or on one side of the stems. All are spreading, to some degree, preferring moisture in a variety of situations from damp meadows to open water. The more aggressive types cover extremely large areas under suitable wetland conditions, where their densely packed stems and roots act as both valuable habitat and natural filtration system. Rushes remain evergreen in mild climates and become semi-evergreen in cold areas. Widely distributed in temperate regions.

Juncus acutus subsp. *Leopoldii*

syn *Juncus acutus* subsp. *sphaerocarpus*
SPINY RUSH

Stiff, spiny stems strongly radiate from a central clump to create a distinctive rounded sphere of green. Very drought-tolerant once established but prefers water and open sunny conditions. The common name comes from the sharply tipped leaves, with which it is best to avoid close contact. From North America, South America and Africa. To 1.2 m (4 ft.). Z8.

Juncus effusus

COMMON RUSH, SOFT RUSH

Probably the most commonly seen rush, both in gardens and in habitat, with light to dark green, comparatively smooth lax stems (hence its common name of soft rush). Found growing in a wide range of places, from bogs to woods and pasture, though generally preferring some degree of moisture. Individually spreading clumps can make large, dense stands. Happiest and most extensive in sunny, open conditions but also tolerates some shade and dryness, at least on a seasonal basis. Very variable, it seeds easily and has given rise to many cultivated selections. Widely distributed worldwide. To 1.2 m (4 ft.). Z3.

'Carman's Japanese'. Extremely attractive and refined, with gently curving rounded shiny green stems topped with profuse light green clusters of flowers whose combined weight often enhances the weeping effect. Effective in a pot. To 45 cm (1½ ft.).

'Curly Gold Strike' (also known as. *J.* 'Curly

Jarava ichu

Gold Strike'). A curled version of 'Gold Strike', with similar golden-edged stems with the occasional hint of pinky red. To 10 cm (4 in.).

'Curly-wurly'. A miniature corkscrew version of the species, with dark green, highly coiled stems that form tight mounds. Ideal in pots or as part of smaller water features. Often listed as a cultivated form of *J. decipiens*, which itself is now regarded as a variety of *J. effusus*. To 10 cm (4 in.).

'Gold Strike'. Has upright stems with bright yellow lines on otherwise darker green stems. To 45 cm (1½ ft.).

var. *spiralis*. The corkscrew rush, well named for its mass of tangled and twisted mid green stems producing clumps that are often noticeably wider than high. To 45 cm (1½ ft.).

Juncus ensifolius
SWORD LEAF RUSH
Forms tight clumps of flat light green leaves, with

ornamental dark reddish brown to purple-black rounded flowers in summer. Prefers sun and moist or marginal conditions, and is especially useful on the side of garden ponds. From North America and Japan. To 40 cm (16 in.). Z5.

Juncus inflexus
HARD RUSH
Resembles the soft rush in many respects, but has much stiffer and often shorter upright stems varying in colour from grey-green to distinct glaucous blue. Noticeably more drought-tolerant than the soft rush, but happy in wet, boggy, open conditions where spreading clumps can form large masses. The pith found in the hollow stems was used as wick for oil lamps and even candles. Comes easily from seed. Widely distributed. To 60 cm (2 ft.). Z4.

'Afro'. Twisted and curled lighter green stems mark this shorter-growing selection that is mostly wider than high. Comes reasonably true from seed. To 30 cm (1 ft.).

'Lovesick Blues'. Comparatively lax stems form pendulous rounded mounds of blue-grey. To 40 cm (16 in.).

Juncus patens
CALIFORNIA GRAY RUSH
Though preferring moist habitats in sun, this attractive grey-leaved upright rush can tolerate extended periods of drought and warm summer temperatures once established. Forming dense clumps over time, especially with plentiful moisture, this attractive plant is often represented by one of several excellent cultivars. Makes a great container plant. From the U.S. West Coast. To 60 cm (2 ft.). Z7.

'Carman's Gray'. An especially grey-stemmed selection found by Ed Carman in California.

'Elk Blue'. Forms compact clumps with an

Juncus patens 'Elk Blue'

attractive blue-grey colouration that is most distinct in full sun.

Koeleria

HAIR GRASS

Found in open, often dry habitats, these annual and perennial cool-season grasses are mostly clump forming. Though wider-leaved, in some ways they resemble the popular mounding fescues, sharing their myriad shades of grey-green foliage. Can be short-lived in gardens, but usually set seed easily. Widely distributed in temperate regions.

Koeleria glauca

syn *Poa glauca*

BLUE HAIR GRASS

Grey-blue leaves on tidy rounded mounds make this species useful for dry, open, sunny sites, though in warmer areas spring flowering is often followed by summer closedown. Foliage will remain in better condition in cooler climates, and can be cut back to stimulate a fresh crop. Often used in drifts or even meadows, individual plants can be short lived but are easily replaced by self-seeders under the right conditions. From Asia and Eurasia. To 60 cm (2 ft.). Z6.

Koeleria macrantha

syn *Koeleria cristata*

CRESTED HAIR GRASS

Bright green clump-forming foliage supports strongly upright stems and light-coloured flowers that have a distinctive presence in prairies and open grasslands. Prefers sunny well-drained soils. Useful for 'no mow' or low-maintenance lawns. From North America and Eurasia. To 60 cm (2 ft.). Z6.

Koeleria pyramidata

PYRAMIDAL HAIR GRASS

Forms bluish green clumps of slowly spreading flattened foliage with tall upright flower spikes that quickly fade to an attractive strawy beige, effective over a long period. Prefers sunny open positions. From temperate North America, Asia and Eurasia. To 90 cm (3 ft.). Z6.

Leymus

LYME GRASS, WILD RYE

These cool-season perennials are often found in the testing conditions of coastal areas, in shifting soils and sands where their rapidly moving root systems are an essential stabilizing influence, and their tough glaucous-to-blue foliage is a further adaptation to such coastal conditions as sea spray and salt-laden winds. Often grown in gardens specifically for their blue leaves. Widely distributed in north temperate regions. Several grasses previously regarded as members of the *Elymus* family such as *E. cinereus*, *E. condensatus*, *E. mollis* and *E. racemosus* have now been reclassified under *Leymus*.

Leymus arenarius

syn *Leymus arenarius* 'Glaucus'

EUROPEAN DUNE GRASS, LYME GRASS

Long popular in gardens for its glaucous blue leaves and tall wheat-like flowers of a similar colouration. A major constituent of coastal sand dunes, where its rapidly moving root system allows it to thrive in the constantly shifting ground which it eventually helps to stabilize, in concert with other beach grasses such as marram, *Ammophila arenaria*. Tough and durable, it is often used in public plantings under difficult conditions such as traffic islands and parking areas. Prefers sun and well-drained poor soils. From northern and western Europe and the U.K.

Leaves to 60 cm (2 ft.) with flowers extending to 1.2 m (4 ft.). Z6.

'Findhorn'. A selection from Scotland, less invasive with a noticeably smaller, more compact habit. To 45 cm (1½ ft.).

Leymus cinereus
syn *Elymus cinereus*
GREY WILD RYE
With grey-green foliage on erect stems and a less spreading habit than *L. arenarius*. Often found at higher elevations through its range, preferring meadows, open woodland and even streamsides. Best in sun and relatively cool summer temperatures, making a good substitute for giant wild rye in colder areas. From North America. To 2.4 m (8 ft.). Z5.

Leymus condensatus
syn *Elymus condensatus*
GIANT WILD RYE
Large slowly spreading clumps of wide, glaucous green to grey leaves support very tall soaring, stiffly upright flower stems. Prefers sloping dry sunny areas and open woodland. Self-seeds when happy. From North America. To 2.7 m (9 ft.). Z7.

'Canyon Prince'. Introduced by the Santa Barbara Botanic Garden this relatively compact selection makes a first-class garden plant with tall upright flower spikes arising from bright silvery grey foliage that intensifies almost to blue in full sun conditions. Happy in most soils except boggy. To 1.5 m (5 ft.).

Leymus mollis
syn *Elymus mollis*
AMERICAN DUNE GRASS
A coastal species that occupies much the same niche as its European counterpart, *L. arenarius*, though more upright and with less blue leaf colour. An important stabilizer of sand dunes. From coastal North America. To 1.2 m (4 ft.). Z3.

Leymus racemosus
syn *Elymus glaucus, Elymus racemosus*
GIANT BLUE RYE
Similar in many respects to *L. arenarius* and often confused with it in gardens. Can exhibit particularly blue foliage on gradually spreading mounds. Best in full sun and not-too-wet soils. From Eurasia. To 1.2 m (4 ft.). Z5.

Leymus triticoides
CREEPING WILD RYE
Preferring relatively moist conditions such as meadows, this strongly spreading species has rather greener leaves than others and is often used for bank stabilization or in re-vegetation schemes where its tolerance of alkaline and saline conditions is especially valuable. Can retain green foliage through the warmer summer periods. From North America. To 90 cm (3 ft.). Z4.

'Shell Creek'. A first-class selection by Dave Fross. Compact, and with a distinct blue-grey colouration to its leaves. To 45 cm (1½ ft.).

Luzula
WOOD RUSH
These evergreen, grass-like wood rushes are actually related to the rushes, *Juncus* species, but bear little actual resemblance. With broad, flattened leaves, they produce dense rosettes of slowly spreading foliage that can make large dense patches over time. Widely distributed in northern-hemisphere cool and temperate regions.

Luzula acuminata

HAIRY WOOD RUSH

Deep green, slowly spreading, basal rosettes of foliage that cope with the tough conditions of woodland and shady places make this quietly attractive species widespread throughout its range. In late spring, relatively insignificant flower spikes appear above fresh green leaves. Useful for shady woodland plantings in association with spring bulbs. From North America. To 40 cm (16 in.). Z4.

Luzula nivea

SNOWY WOOD RUSH

Slowly increasing mounds of frequently toothed-edged dark green leaves are covered in tiny white hairs, creating a light grey to white 'snowy' appearance. Tolerates a variety of soils from very damp to often-dry. Happiest in part shade rather than full sun. Covered with spikes of tiny white to cream-coloured flowers in late spring. Comes easily from seed. From Eurasia. To 60 cm (2 ft.). Z6.

Luzula sylvatica

GREATER WOOD RUSH

Widespread and common throughout its wide range, this tough and adaptable species is found in a variety of habitats including woodlands, moorlands and most damp places. Happy in different degrees of shade but will tolerate some sun. The largest wood rush, with wide leaves on rosettes that can cover significant areas of dense weed-proof cover. The flowers, produced in spring, are relatively insignificant as with most wood rushes. Comes easily from seed and has

Leymus racemosus

given rise to many different cultivars. From Eurasia and the U.K. To 45 cm (1½ ft.). Z4.

'Aurea'. One of the brightest and most effective forms through winter and especially in spring, when the rosettes of wide leaves are at their brightest golden yellow. Best sited in light shade as the delicate leaves are liable to burn in strong sunlight.

'Hohe Tatra'. The true form has the widest leaves (up to 2.5 cm [1 in.]) of any of the wood sedges but is often confused with 'Aurea' in gardens.

'Marginata'. An old cultivar, with leaves narrowly margined in creamy white.

'Taggart's Cream'. Some new growth is almost white before gradually fading to green.

Luzula sylvatica 'Aurea'. Photograph courtesy of Dianna Jazwinski.

Melica
MELIC

A large group of invaluable (if sometimes unassuming) clump-forming deciduous grasses for both shady woodland and sunny open sites. Being cool-season growers this group is especially valuable during early spring, with many shutting down or becoming summer-dormant with increasing dryness.

Melica altissima
SIBERIAN MELIC

An upright leafy species often represented by the white form 'Alba' or the purple form 'Atropurpurea', which both come reasonably true from seed and are used in mostly sunny open areas, though they will tolerate some light shade in reasonable soils. At best in the early part of the year; cutting down after the first flush of flower has finished can stimulate a second crop of flower. Can self-seed lightly. From Central and Eastern Europe. To 1.2 m (4 ft.). Z5.

Melica californica
CALIFORNIAN MELIC

Native to a variety of conditions and soils, from sunny slopes to almost-damp woodlands. Bright green clumps of foliage produce narrow spikes of initially white flowers that fade and remain intact as the grass enters summer dormancy in drier areas. From California. To 90 cm (3 ft.). Z8.

Melica imperfecta
COAST MELIC, FOOTHILL MELIC

Arguably less showy than other melics, this adaptable species is found in woodlands, dry hillsides and even coastal dunes where its delicate upright appearance is often melded in a wider matrix of native grasses such as *Nassella*, *Koeleria* and *Poa*. Understated, and perhaps underestimated, it plays an important role in meadows and woodland gardens. Equally attractive in summer dormancy. Will seed easily when happy. From southern California. To 60 cm (2 ft.). Z8.

Melica uniflora

WOOD MELIC

Usually represented in gardens by one of the following forms, the species has dainty bright green leaves on gradually spreading rootstock with small, sparse purplish brown flowers. To 60 cm (2 ft). Z5.

'Alba'. With dainty grain-like white flowers that contract effectively with fresh green foliage. Especially useful in gardens during the earlier part of the season in shady areas and quiet corners.

'Variegata'. Pretty with green-and-white-striped foliage. A little more compact than the species.

Melinis

syn *Rhynchelytrum*

PINK CRYSTALS, RUBY GRASS

Aptly named for their pretty pink flowers, these warm-season, usually evergreen grasses contain some species such as *Melinis repens* that are considered noxious weeds in warm climates where they have become naturalized. Requiring full sun, they are very drought tolerant and well adapted to dry environments.

Melinis nerviglumis

PINK CRYSTALS, RUBY GRASS

The common name of pink crystals accurately describes the appearance of this attractive species' bright pink flowers, produced from tidy mounds of grey-green foliage provided the plant is given sufficient protection and a head start in colder areas. Drought-tolerant but cold-tender. To 60 cm (2 ft.). From southern Africa. Z9.

Melica uniflora 'Variegata'. Photograph courtesy of Dianna Jazwinski.

Melinis nerviglumis. Photograph courtesy of Dianna Jazwinski.

Milium

WOOD MILLET

Common in mostly open woodland but occasionally found in sunnier areas, these cool-season deciduous grasses are usually represented in gardens by *Milium effusum*.

Milium effusum

WOOD MILLET

At best in spring with adequate shade and moisture, the clump-forming wood millets can go dormant during the drier summer months but will remain active with enough moisture. Once the initial flush of spring growth is over, cutting back old foliage can stimulate a second period of activity. Will seed when happy and are frequently used in gardens as one of the following forms.

Milium effusum 'Yaffle'. Photograph courtesy of Dianna Jazwinski.

From much of the temperate northern hemisphere. Z5.

'Aureum'. Of uncertain garden origin, Bowles' golden grass is perhaps the best-known form, with delicate clumps of foliage, stems and flowers all coloured a uniform, clear golden yellow which may appear pale green in areas of deeper shade. Although difficult from seed, it comes true and will seed around lightly if conditions are to its liking. To 60 cm (2 ft.).

'Yaffle'. A more recent selection, with mid green leaves having a very distinctive narrow golden yellow central line. In spring, golden yellow flowers are held high above the foliage. To 60 cm (2 ft).

Miscanthus

EULALIA GRASS, JAPANESE SILVER GRASS, SUSUKI ZOKU

Miscanthus has long held a deep fascination for gardeners. Many of the oldest cultivars were selected in Japan where these warm-season deciduous grasses are traditionally regarded as a symbol of autumn. In the West, long before grasses became more widely known and accepted, miscanthus forms such as 'Zebrinus' were used by keen Victorian gardeners as 'dot' or specimen plants in formal annual bedding displays. Today, although their use has been rightly tempered in areas such as the southeastern United States where conditions can allow copious seeding, they remain valuable garden plants in all other areas where they do not seed aggressively.

Almost unequalled in the grass family for their sheer range of size, flower and leaf colour, they are tough, generally long-lived plants needing little maintenence in return for a very long season of interest. Although generally preferring open sunny positions, some—especially the variegated *M. sinensis* forms—will grow well in partial shade.

Soils can vary from fairly dry to distinctly wet though the plants appear to tolerate the wettest soils only if accompanied by commensurate high-sunlight hours.

Depending on their height, miscanthus can be effectively used as screening, as informal hedges and especially in larger plantings where their bulk and flower-power combine well with so many other plants including larger perennials such as *Eupatorium*, *Aster*, *Rudbeckia*, *Verbena* and *Veronicastrum*.

Miscanthus floridulus
GIANT MISCANTHUS

Rare in gardens, this clump-forming species can reach 2.4 m (8 ft.). Often, plants mislabelled as *M. floridulus* in Western gardens are actually *M. ×giganteus*. True *M. floridulus* is distinguishable by its coarse wide foliage and narrow flower. From southern Japan, Taiwan and the Pacific Islands. Z7.

Miscanthus ×giganteus
GIANT MISCANTHUS

A most useful hybrid between *Miscanthus sacchariflorus* and *Miscanthus sinensis*, with some of the best attributes of both. Bright, clear green, slightly pendulous foliage hang as a fountain from sturdy tall stems making this plant one of the most distinctive of all miscanthus. Clump-forming, it is often used as an informal screen or shelter planting or in association with other bold plants as part of a border. Flowers only after extended summer periods, and then does not produce fertile seed. From Japan. To 3 m (10 ft). Z4.

Miscanthus ×giganteus

Miscanthus nepalensis

HIMALAYAN FAIRY GRASS

Distinctive for its compact mounds of foliage and gold, braid-like, non-fading flowers, produced on dainty stems held high above the leaves. Has been proving hardier than expected in sheltered well-drained positions in relatively cold areas. Comes easily from seed. From Nepal. To 1.5 m (5 ft.). Z8–9 (and possibly colder).

Miscanthus oligostachyus

KARI YASU MODOKI

Rather small and very cold-hardy. Though compact in habit with diminutive, less-than-showy flowers, it can be very effective en masse. Will tolerate some shade and can offer yellow-brown fall colour. Several variegated forms have been selected in Japan, with *M. o.* 'Nanus Variegatus' most often encountered in Western gardens. Seldom self- sows. From Japan. To 1.2 m (4 ft.). Z4.

Miscanthus nepalensis. Photograph courtesy of Dianna Jazwinski.

Miscanthus 'Purpurascens'

syn *Miscanthus sinensis* var. *purpurascens*

AUTUMN FLAME MISCANTHUS

Of uncertain parentage and history; possibly a hybrid with *M. oligostachyus*. Its short stature, bright fall colour and reluctance to set fertile seed make it an excellent garden plant. In areas with shorter summers such as the U.K. it seldom flowers and is known only for its flame-coloured autumnal leaves. From Japan. To 1.5 m (5 ft.). Z4.

Miscanthus sacchariflorus

SILVER BANNER GRASS

Very similar in garden terms to *M.* ×*giganteus*, and as one parent often mistaken for it, this species differs in its running rootstock and ability to set viable seed from early flowering in warm areas. In cooler climates the running habit is slowed to a gentle jog and it frequently fails to flower as the growing season is too short. From Japan, Korea and China. To 3 m (10 ft.). Z4.

'Gotemba'. Similar to the species in habit but a little less robust, with very attractive golden yellow-striped foliage that has never been seen to flower. To 2.1 m (7 ft.).

Miscanthus sinensis

EULALIA, SILVER GRASS, SUSUKI

The classic *Miscanthus* species from which most garden cultivars have arisen. Pretty much all are clump forming, offering an exhaustive range of height, flower and leaf colour. All have a generally rounded outline, usually taller than wide, with flower produced en masse, level with or above the foliage's final height. Viable seed is produced by many of the cultivars which, if sown, will revert to the species—which itself is widely variable from seed. From China, Korea and Japan. Variable to 2.4 m (8 ft.). Z5–6.

'Abundance'. An outstanding form, making

wonderful dense mounds of attractive narrow leaves covered in masses of delicate buff-white flowers. One of the very best miscanthus for general garden use. 'Abundance' is a recent cultivar name, given by Knoll Gardens, intended to identify this specific form. To 1.5 m (5 ft.).

'Afrika'. Seldom seem, and highly valued for its wonderful red foliage turning noticeably earlier in the season than most other miscanthus. Shorter, a little less vigorous than many and therefore extremely desirable. To 1.5 m (5 ft.).

'Andante'. A striking Kurt Bluemel selection from the United States, possibly with *M. transmorrisonensis* as one parent. Very special-looking with beautiful pink inflorescences held clear above mounds of green foliage. To 2.1 m (7 ft.).

'China'. An excellent form, with narrow dark green foliage, tall long-stemmed red flower plumes and vibrant autumn colour. Often confused with 'Ferner Osten' from which it differs only in flower detail. To 1.8 m (6 ft.).

'Cindy'. A new, compact selection from Knoll Gardens with many dainty, semi-pendulous, soft pinky red flowers held clear above the compact foliage. To 1.5 m (5 ft.).

'Dixieland'. Slightly more compact than 'Variegatus' , with rather wonderful narrow fresh green and white variegated foliage. Ideal in tubs or where a smaller plant is needed. Happy in partial shade. To 1.8 m (6 ft.).

'Dronning Ingrid'. With distinctive dark red upright flowers and foliage that is frequently purple-tinted often before turning vibrant autumnal colours. To 1.8 m (6 ft.).

Miscanthus sinensis 'Abundance'

'Elfin'. An outstanding form, making wonderful mounds of attractive narrow leaves covered in masses of light pinky white flowers and distinctive red stems. Previously one of a group of 'Yakushima Dwarf' seedlings 'Elfin' is a recent cultivar name, given by Knoll Gardens, intended to identify this specific form. To 1.5 m (5 ft.).

'Emmanuel Lepage'. Highly likeable, with an attractive loose habit and deep pinky red flowers held clear above the foliage from high summer onwards. To 2.1 m (7 ft.).

'Etincelle'. A zebra grass, with yellow cross-banding on the thin leaves which form pleasing rounded mounds of foliage. Plumes of silvery flowers are held above the leaves in late summer. To 1.5 m (5 ft.).

'Ferner Osten'. A superb selection and one of the best for general garden use, forming mounds of narrow foliage turning bright copper and red in autumn. Spectacular very dark red flower plumes. To 1.8 m (6 ft.).

'Flamingo'. A first-class cultivar, with many strikingly elegant, slightly pendent dark pinkish flower plumes in late summer and good autumn colour. To 1.8 m (6 ft.).

'Gewitterwolke'. Forms superb upright clumps of relatively wide dark green leaves topped with many striking dark pink flower plumes from summer onwards. To 2.1 m (7 ft.).

'Gold Bar'. A recent addition to the zebra grass family, its yellow banding appearing almost simultaneously with the spring foliage on compact plants. To 90 cm (3 ft.).

'Goliath'. As its name suggests, one of the tallest-flowering miscanthus, with an excellent habit and lots of pinky red flowers on stems that tower above most other plants. To 2.7 m (9 ft.).

'Gracillimus'. An old, established cultivar grown principally for its fine-textured foliage that forms gracefully rounded mounds bleaching to pale straw colour for a winter feature. To 2.1 m (7 ft.).

'Gracillimus Nanus'. A very new, compact form of the popular 'Gracillimus', having a similar habit though noticeably shorter in all respects. Tends to produce soft pinky red flowers. To 1.5 m (5 ft.).

'Graziella'. Attractive silver flowers open in late summer high above the narrow green foliage, which can turn a vivid rich copper red and orange autumn colour. To 1.8 m (6 ft.).

'Haiku'. An Ernst Pagels selection, with a generally upright habit and gracefully pendulous pink flowers from late summer onwards. To 2 m (6 ft.).

'Hermann Müssel'. A superb Pagels introduction having strongly upright stems topped with pinky brown flowers that are held some distance above the foliage, giving a distinctive appearance. To 2.1 m (7 ft.).

'Huron Sunrise'. A Canadian selection, characterized by red-tinted flowers late in the season. To 2.1 m (7 ft.). Z4.

'Kaskade'. Grown for its slightly pendent, large,

Miscanthus sinensis 'Cindy'

loosely opened pink-tinted inflorescences with a narrowly upright habit. To 2.1 m (7 ft.).

'Kleine Fontäne'. A first-class plant, forming mounds of narrow green foliage and many soft pink flowers in summer which later gradually fade beige. To 1.8 m (6 ft.).

'Kleine Silberspinne'. Elegant needle-like green foliage forms distinct compact rounded mounds with masses of beautiful silky red silver flowers from late summer onwards. To 1.8 m (6 ft.).

'Little Kitten'. A comparatively dwarf selection, making strong clumps of narrow green foliage on compact mounds. To 1.2 m (4 ft.).

'Little Zebra'. A new, possibly more regular-flowering, compact form of zebra grass with yellow bands topped with wine red flowers in late summer. To 1.5 m (5 ft.).

'Malepartus'. The original standard by which other cultivars were judged—and still good today, with striking columns of silver-veined broad foliage and flowerheads of the darkest purple-red, fading silver. To 2.1 m (7 ft.).

'Morning Light'. Perfectly named, with upright stems and gracefully arching fine-textured cream and green foliage giving this form an unequalled lightness. Topped with perfectly matched pinkish flowers in good years. Refined and elegant in pots or by the water's edge. To 1.8 m (6 ft.).

'Nippon'. An excellent relatively compact form, with strongly upright clumps of narrow foliage and fantastic early-flowering red plumes with occasional orange-red autumn tinted foliage. To 1.5 m (5 ft.).

Miscanthus sinensis 'Hermann Müssel'

'Positano'. Strong mounds of arching green foliage produce lovely red flowers from midsummer onwards. Good autumn colour. To 2.1 m (7 ft.).

'Professor Richard Hansen'. A distinctive Pagels selection with broad green leaves topped by tall upright flowers, red at first before turning beige-white, which are held well clear of the foliage. To 2.4 m (8 ft.).

'Red Spear'. Tall, strongly upright stems produce flower buds reminiscent of spear heads until the point of opening, when they change into bright red inflorescences still facing skywards. A Knoll Gardens selection. To 2.4 m (8 ft.).

'Rigoletto'. Possibly the most compact white variegated form, selected by Kurt Bluemel in the United States. To 1.5 m (5 ft.).

'Roland'. An elegant cultivar and one of the tallest, with beautiful pink-tinted inflorescences held on tall stems from midsummer onwards. To 2.7 m (9 ft.).

'Roterpfeil'. Selected by Pagels and named for its upright slow-growing habit. Produces pinky red flowers and red foliage early in the season. To 1.5 m (5 ft.).

'Rotsilber'. Forms wonderful mounds of bright green leaves and many striking deep pinky red flower plumes from summer onwards. Orange-red autumn colour. To 1.8 m (6 ft.).

'Sarabande'. Fine, narrow white-striped green foliage forms statuesque mounds topped with golden copper inflorescences from late summer onwards. To 2.1 m (7 ft.).

'Silberfeder'. An old, established form making tall upright stems of deep green foliage with distinct silver midrib, and large silver-pink flower plumes in late summer. To 2.1 m (7 ft.).

'Strictus'. Erect clumps of spiky green foliage with striking yellow cross banding are topped with pinky red flowers in late summer. More

Miscanthus sinensis 'Little Kitten'

Miscanthus sinensis 'Red Spear'

Miscanthus sinensis 'Roterpfeil'

upright and possibly a little shorter than 'Zebrinus'. To 2.1 m (7 ft.).

'Undine'. Mounds of narrow white-veined leaves with beautiful deep pinky purple flowers turn magnificently light and fluffy late in the season. To 2.1 m (7 ft.).

'Variegatus'. Very distinctive with strongly green-and-white-striped leaves on upright stems. One of the brightest 'whites' that will tolerate some shade. To 2.1 m (7 ft.).

'Yakushima Dwarf'. Known by a variety of similar names, this is not a clonal cultivar but a name given to several very similar, originally seed-raised plants from the Japanese island of Yakushima. While most forms are excellent garden plants, several of the best forms have been given specific cultivar names in order to avoid continued confusion; see *Miscanthus* 'Abundance', *M*. 'Elfin' and *M*. 'Little Kitten'.

'Zebrinus'. A zebra grass having tall bright green stems with striking yellow-banded foliage, and occasionally producing copper-tinted flowers. To 2.1 m (7 ft.).

'Zwergelefant'. The most amazing crinkled pinkish flowers are produced in an initially trunk-like shape while emerging from the upright

Miscanthus sinensis 'Zwergelefant'

stems—so unique-looking that the comparatively coarse foliage seems irrelevant. To 2.1 m (7 ft.).

Miscanthus sinensis var. *condensatus*
syn *Miscanthus condensatus*
HACHIJO SUSUKI

A variety principally distinguished by its quietly attractive stems covered in a whitish bloom. Has given rise to several excellent variegated cultivars.

Produces reddish flowers late in the season most years. From Japan, China, Korea and the Pacific Islands. To 2.1 m (7 ft., and occasionally taller when in flower). Z5.

'Cabaret'. Among the most striking of variegated plants, with wide ribbon-like foliage marked with unusual creamy white centres and darker green margins forming sturdy upright clumps. Pinky red flowers are only produced in warm summers.

'Cosmo Revert'. A form that has reverted back from the variegated version, which it is apt to do.

'Cosmopolitan'. Upright clumps of wide ribbon-like foliage with deep green centres and creamy white margins make for a striking foliage effect. Occasional red flowers emerge in late summer. Like most variegated miscanthus, it tolerates partial shade.

Miscanthus transmorrisonensis

TAIWAN GRASS

An attractive species, producing flowers on tall willowy stems held some distance above the foliage on the best forms. Often regarded as evergreen though only in comparatively mild climates, it comes easily from seed but is inclined to be very variable in habit this way. From Taiwan. To 2.1 m (7 ft.). Z6–7.

'Ferndown'. Recently selected for its upright habit and comparatively large flowers held high about the wide green foliage.

Molinia

MOOR GRASS, PURPLE MOOR GRASS

Widespread and common throughout most of their Eurasian range, these cool-season deciduous grasses can be found in a variety of habitats, from boggy moors to relatively dry heathlands, and bring their same tough and adaptable qualities to the garden. Reliably clump-forming

and cold-hardy, the clear, strongly linear generally upright line of the flower stems is probably the chief attraction; when seen in full autumn gold colouration, and especially when highlighted by sunshine, it is quite simply breathtaking. Preferring sunny open positions, they will tolerate some light shade in higher-sunlight areas.

Moor grasses, especially the shorter forms, are practical matrix grasses for open meadows and are also good in mixed plantings where they act as a foil for other more solid partners including perennials like sedums, sanguisorbas and persicarias. The airy transparent nature of the flower stems of the taller forms in particular make moor grasses ideal for internal screens and alternative 'hedges'. Only one species is cultivated: *Molinia caerulea*, which is split into two subspecies depending primarily on the height of the flowers.

'Autumn Charm'. A selection by Ross Humphrey, chosen for its noticeably upright habit and warm brown autumnal stems that are among the tallest of *Molinia* selections. To 1.2 m (4 ft.). Z4–5.

Molinia caerulea subsp. *arundinacea*

syn *Molinia altissima, Molinia arundinacea, Molinia litoralis*

TALL PURPLE MOOR GRASS

The taller of the two subspecies, and just as robust, this moor grass is among the most graceful of grasses. Relatively large mounds of bright green foliage support airy stems that reach upwards, mostly in an ever-widening arc. Unlike shorter forms, tall moor grass is perhaps best given some individual space to take advantage of its refined shape—for instance, as a specimen towering over much shorter companions. Tall stems will usually collapse under their own weight before the end of the winter. From Eurasia. To 2.4 m (8 ft.). Z4–5.

'Bergfreund'. A recent selection, in some ways similar to the long-established 'Transparent', with tidy mounds of foliage and slightly shorter open and airy inflorescences all turning orange and yellow in autumn. To 1.8 m (6 ft.).

'Cordoba'. Unusual, with strong, graceful, gently curving flower stems and good honey-gold colour. To 2.1 m (7 ft.).

'Karl Foerster'. One of the best cultivars, with outstanding golden brown flower spikes turning a superb butter yellow colour in autumn. To 2.1 m (7 ft.).

'Skyracer'. Selected by American nurseryman Kurt Bluemel. Strongly upright and particularly tall, turning the usual warm autumnal colours. To 2.4 m (8 ft.).

'Transparent'. A long-established cultivar, aptly named for its airy, see-through inflorescences. To 1.8 m (6 ft.).

'Windsaule'. Strongly upright, with flower panicles a little more slender than some. Excellent as a specimen plant. To 2.1 m (7 ft.).

'Windspiel'. Tall clumps wave airily in the slightest breeze, high above mounds of graceful foliage that turns a stunning honey colour in autumn. To 2.1 m (7 ft.).

'Zuneigung'. Distinctly elegant, with tall slender stems and heavy arching panicles of flower swaying in the slightest breeze. To 1.8 m (6 ft.).

Molinia caerulea subsp. *caerulea*

PURPLE MOOR GRASS

Commonly referred to as simply *M. caerulea*, plants belonging to this group have flower stems

Molinia caerulea subsp. *arundinacea* 'Karl Foerster'

usually below 1.2 m (4 ft.) tall. Coming easily from seed, the resulting variation has produced a number of good cultivars, nearly all of which follow the same broad outline, producing a tidy clump of thin bright green leaves from which arise the narrow dainty stems topped with masses of tiny, initially purple flowers. Airy to the point of invisibility at first, their sculptural qualities improve as the flowers age and the season progresses. Arguably at their brightest during the autumn when stems and leaves take on a golden glow, they fade gradually with the changing seasons but retain a distinctive habit throughout the winter. From Eurasia. Z4–5.

'Dauerstrahl'. Seldom seen, with dark purplish flowers held in an upright to gently arching habit. To 90 cm (3 ft.).

'Edith Dudszus'. Selected for its initially rich purple (almost black) flower stems and dense flower spikes, profusely produced from tussocks of good green foliage. To 1.2 m (4 ft.).

'Heidebraut'. An infrequently seen, relatively upright form with flower stems that gradually arch outwards as they gain in height. To 1.2 m (4 ft.).

'Moorflamme'. Compact mounds of green foliage develop rich purple autumn hues, and upright dark flower stems turn a wonderful orange in winter. To 90 cm (3 ft.).

'Moorhexe'. Forms compact clumps of green leaves and strongly vertical architectural flower spikes. To 90 cm (3 ft.).

'Poul Petersen'. Forms strong clumps of striking, reasonably upright stems—particularly effective en masse. To 90 cm (3 ft.).

'Strahlenquelle'. Not often encountered, the true form of this unusual cultivar is widely arching and needs space to display its spreading flower stems. To 90 cm (3 ft.).

'Variegata'. A good, compact grass, with low tufts of bright, well-marked green and cream leaves and many striking, arching buff plumes in autumn. To 90 cm (3 ft.).

Muhlenbergia

MUHLY

Until recently much underused, these warm-season, mostly clump-forming grasses are durable, adaptable and very beautiful. Thriving in drought-prone sun-baked conditions in their native habitats, they are especially useful for gardens in warmer climates but can survive in much cooler areas provided soils are well drained.

Muhlenbergia capillaris

PINK MUHLY

Spectacular when in flower: masses of vibrant pink, cloud-like flowers obscure the basal mounds of relatively drab foliage, making the whole plant visible from some distance. Wide-ranging and variable from seed, the species has given rise to several cultivars including a white form (' White Cloud'). Requires long sunlight hours to flower successfully. From Mexico, the southeastern U.S. and the West Indies. Z6–7. To 90 cm (3 ft.).

Muhlenbergia dumosa

BAMBOO MUHLY

Different from most other family members; grown principally for its gracefully curving bamboo-like stems that support billowing masses of cloud-like tiny green foliage dotted with occasional pale yellow flowers. Evergreen in warmer areas with enough moisture, it will drop its leaves in severe drought or during the winter period in cooler climates. From the southern U.S. and Mexico. To 1.2 m (4 ft.). Z8.

Muhlenbergia lindheimeri

LINDHEIMER'S MUHLY

With basal clumps of attractive blue-grey leaves that tolerate hot, dry conditions and even a little shade in high-sunlight areas. Tall, upright stems of lighter grey flower spikes are especially effective later in the season as a vertical accent in the plant border. From Texas and Mexico. To 1.5 m (5 ft.). Z6–7.

Muhlenbergia rigens

DEER GRASS

Established clumps have a memorable, architectural almost-pincushion-like effect wherever it can be grown successfully. At home in warm drought-prone areas, but also able to perform well in much cooler climates provided it has a sunny well-drained position. Whether massed or as individuals, enough space should be left around each plant for the development of its stunning outline. From the southern U.S. and Mexico. To 1.5 m (5 ft.). Z6–7.

Nassella

NEEDLE GRASS

These mostly perennial clump-forming cool-season grasses come from open, sunny areas. Their collective common name refers to the distinctive needle-like flowers that are a major part of their attraction and which can set prolific seed. The three Californian species are ideal in meadows. Many of these species were previously included in the genus *Stipa* and are still regarded as such by many authorities.

Nassella cernua

syn *Stipa cernua*

NODDING NEEDLE GRASS

Found in open grassland, chaparral and open woodland. Clump-forming with narrow green leaves in spring, followed by distinctly nodding reddish purple needle-like flowers that gradually dry, the whole plant becoming summer-dormant and then re-awakening with the arrival of the autumn rains. Seeds easily and is a popular

Muhlenbergia dumosa

Muhlenbergia rigens

choice for erosion control and in public plantings. Dislikes summer water while in dormancy. From California. To 90 cm (3 ft.). Z8.

Nassella lepida
syn *Stipa lepida*
FOOTHILL NEEDLE GRASS
Very similar to *N. cernua* but with narrower leaves, flowers with a less pronounced nodding habit and a greater tolerance for some shade. From California. To 90 cm (3 ft.). Z8.

Nassella neesiana
syn *Stipa neesiana*
CHILEAN NEEDLE GRASS
Prefers well-drained, sunny positions though its ability to seed heavily limits its use in more sensitive areas. From South America. To 90 cm (3 ft.). Z8.

Nassella pulchra
syn *Stipa pulchra*
PURPLE NEEDLE GRASS
Found in dry grasslands and scrub, this delicately beautiful flower has especially long purple needle-like flowers in spring that quickly dry silver beige when fading into summer dormancy. Dispossessed of much of its original range by introduced exotics, it is now the official state grass of California where it is still widespread in sunny well-drained areas. From California. To 90 cm (3 ft.). Z8.

Nassella tenuissima
syn *Stipa tenuissima*
MEXICAN FEATHER GRASS
Arguably one of the most popular and commonly planted of all grasses. Clump-forming and easy-growing, with bright mid green, narrow, hair-like

Nassella tenuissima

foliage topped by initially light green flowers that quickly fade beige, produced so profusely that they weigh the whole plant down. Short-lived, but sets seed easily or can be divided with equal facility to maintain vigour. Drought-tolerant and happy in full sun, but dislikes wet soils. From the southern U.S. through South America. To 60 cm (2 ft.). Z7.

Nassella trichotoma

syn *Stipa trichotoma*

SERRATED TUSSOCK GRASS

Forms neat mounds of fine hair-like foliage covered with hazy, delicately structured flowers. Requires full sun and well-drained soils. Popular in colder climates, its ability to set seed in warmer climates has relegated this grass to a noxious weed in parts of the United States and Australia. From South America. To 45 cm ($1\frac{1}{2}$ ft.). Z8.

Ophiopogon

LILY GRASS, MONDO GRASS

Unrelated to the grass family (or the lily family), these grass-like evergreens from Asia share a superficial resemblance to grasses due to their narrow strap-like leaves, produced on slowly spreading mounds of tough evergreen foliage. Also reminiscent of *Liriope* with the same deep green strap-like foliage, though lacking the upright spikes of flower.

Ophiopogon japonicus

MONDO GRASS

Creates slowly spreading mounds of tough dark green leaves. Has given rise to a number of cultivated forms including those with silver- or golden-striped variegated leaves, and is commonly seen in the following distinctive form. From Asia, especially Japan. Z6.

'Minor'. A miniature version of the species, with much-smaller evergreen leaves forming tight, very slow-growing clumps. Useful as ground cover and as a lawn replacement in shady situations, though it will only tolerate minimal foot traffic. To 10 cm (4 in.).

Ophiopogon planiscapus

MONDO GRASS

Tough, durable, slowly creeping and perfect for covering the dry, shady areas under trees. Slow to establish it gradually forms low dense weed proof mats of dark green leaves dotted with occasional white flowers and purple black fruits. Seldom needs any attention once established. From Asia. To 15 cm (6 in.). Z6.

'Nigrescens'. Grown for its dramatic black leaves, pinkish white flowers and black fruits. Similarly tough and adaptable to a wide range of conditions, it produces weed-proof mounds

Ophiopogon planiscapus 'Nigrescens'

of strap like foliage over time. Most effective as ground cover in sun or part shade; the black colouration can revert to green in too-deep shade. To 20 cm (8 in.).

Oryzopsis
RICE GRASS

This widespread group comprises more than thirty species of warm-season perennial evergreens—unrelated to the rice plants grown for food and have been included in the genus *Piptatherum*. All re-seed easily and can become serious weeds in sensitive areas.

Oryzopsis miliacea
syn *Piptatherum miliacea*
INDIAN RICE GRASS, SMILO GRASS

Forms very attractive, generally upright clumps of shiny green leaves from which numerous delicate panicles arch upwards and outwards. Prefers

Oryzopsis miliacea. Photograph courtesy of Dianna Jazwinski.

sunny open positions. Can re-seed in most climates and is regarded as a serious weed in many warmer areas. From Asia, Africa and Eurasia. To 1.2 m (4 ft.). Z6.

Panicum
MILLET, PANIC GRASS

The majority of species in this huge group of annual and perennial warm-season deciduous grasses are found in tropical areas. In gardens, the most useful and widespread is *Panicum virgatum* and its many cultivars. Some annual species such as *Panicum milaceum* are popular with gardeners and flower-arrangers for their freely produced, relatively large and airy flowers. Another annual, *Panicum capillare*, is a constituent of some bird food mixtures and is occasionally found in gardens as a result.

Panicum amarum
COAST SWITCH GRASS

A distinctive coastal species, tolerating a wide range of soils and habitats throughout its limited range but preferring sandy soils. Typically more arching than the better-known *Panicum virgatum*, its foliage and flowers combining to create mounds of initially upright stems and leaves that gradually splay outwards as flowers develop and age. Leaves vary from green to blue, and the root system is strongly spreading to clumping. All require sun and not-too-fertile soils for best colour and performance. From the North American coast to Mexico. To 1.5 m (5 ft.). Z5.

var. *amarulum*. A strongly clump-forming botanical variety that can have very silvery blue foliage and a typically cascading habit.

'Dewey Blue'. A beautiful form with exceptionally silvery blue-grey stems and leaves selected from wild seed collected by Rick Darke and Dale Hendricks.

Panicum bulbosum
TEXAS GRASS

Forms clumps of light grey-green foliage that comes from swollen bases, and produces interesting upright stems of reddish flowers drying to a warm beige, which are most effective when used en masse. Provides yellow autumn colour. Seeds under suitable conditions, preferring a sunny open position and not-too-wet soil. From the southern U.S., Mexico and western South America. To 90 cm (3 ft.). Z6–9.

Panicum virgatum
PANIC GRASS, SWITCH GRASS

Long-lived, tough and adaptable, panic grasses rank among the most useful of grasses in our gardens and designed spaces. A main constituent of the once-widespread tall grass prairie, they can be used on a wide variety of soil types from wet to dry, though mostly prefer a sunny open situation. Being so populous, they display much variation in their native habitats but are largely upright-stemmed and clump-forming, with tiny

Panicum amarum var. *amarulum*

Panicum bulbosum. Photograph courtesy of Dianna Jazwinski.

often-purplish flowers held on dainty panicles and produced profusely enough to create a hazy cloud of flower that can virtually obscure the foliage. As with many good garden grasses, heavy rain or snow may bend the taller stems, though most will return to their customary upright stance with the return of better weather. Summer foliage can vary with different forms coloured green to silvery blue, while autumnal foliage colour can vary from yellow through orange to many shades of red and can be highly effective in the garden. Widely distributed in North America. To 2.4 m (8 ft.). Z4.

'Blue Tower'. A really tall blue selection from Greg Speichert, with leaves a distinct glaucous blue. To 2.4 m (8 ft.).

'Cloud Nine'. A truly magnificent selection, tall and airy with wonderful glaucous blue-green foliage, an upright habit and attractive golden autumn colour. To 2.4 m (8 ft.).

'Dallas Blues'. Among the bluest selections, with blue stems, wide leaves, and showy flower panicles on solid upright mounds. To 1.8 m (6 ft.).

'Hänse Herms'. Green leaves take on red tones in summer before turning burgundy in autumn. Particularly valued for its abundant panicles and relaxed habit. To 1.2 m (4 ft.).

'Heavy Metal'. With very distinctive clumps of upright grey-green foliage, large panicles of tiny purplish spikelets in summer and reddish-purple-tinted autumn colour. An eye-catching selection from Kurt Bluemel. To 1.5 m (5 ft.).

'Heiliger Hain'. With soft pinky beige flowers and bluish green foliage that turns a very deep burgundy red in autumn. To 1.2 m (4 ft.).

'Kupferhirse'. Valuable as a vertical accent, topped with warm coppery brown panicles from late summer. Good yellow-orange autumn foliage. To 1.2 m (4 ft.).

'Northwind'. One of few truly upright forms of *P. v.*, having a very distinctive narrow vertical habit and wide blue-grey foliage that turns yellowy orange in autumn. To 1.5 m (5 ft.).

'Prairie Fire'. Selected by Gary and Sandy Trucks for its green foliage that turns deep reddish purple as the season progresses. To 1.2 m (4 ft.).

Panicum virgatum

Panicum virgatum 'Dallas Blues'

Panicum virgatum 'Hänse Herms'

Panicum virgatum 'Heavy Metal'

Panicum virgatum 'Heiliger Hain'

'Prairie Sky'. Introduced by Roger Gettig, with striking blue stems and foliage topped with delicate, airy flowerheads. Stems are mostly upright in poor, well-drained soils. To 1.2 m (4 ft.).

'Red Cloud'. A lovely form, grown specially for its large panicles of conspicuous red spikelets. To 1.5 m (5 ft.).

'Rehbraun'. An older selection with an attractive habit and green leaves turning various shades of wine red in autumn. To 1.2 m (4 ft.).

'Rotstrahlbusch'. Possibly one of the oldest *P. v.* cultivars, with subtle tones of red suffusing the green leaves during autumn. To 1.2 m (4 ft.).

'Shenandoah'. Selected by Hans Simon from seedlings of 'Hanse Herms'. Stunning, with foliage that has dark red tones turning a gorgeous

Panicum virgatum 'Northwind'

wine colour by late summer. Proving to be one of the best for red autumn foliage. To 1.2 m (4 ft.).

'Squaw'. A green-leaved Kurt Bluemel selection with pinky red flowers and autumnal tinted foliage. To 1.2 m (4 ft.).

'Strictum'. Of generally upright habit, with grey-green leaves and relatively large, light, airy panicles of flower. To 1.5 m (5 ft.).

'Warrior'. With green foliage and heads of freely produced purple-tinted flowers. To 1.5 m (5 ft.).

Paspalum

A diverse group of more than three hundred warm-season species, including some used as turf grass in hotter areas.

Paspalum quadrifarium

PASPALUM GRASS

Forms clumps of blue-green leaves topped by slightly arching flower plumes and delicately attractive flowers. Needs a sunny well-drained spot and is often semi-evergreen in cooler areas. From South America. To 1.8 m (6 ft.). Z8–9.

Pennisetum

FOUNTAIN GRASS

Among the most showy of all grasses, with cylindrical, fluffy to smooth, bottlebrush-like flowers in a palette ranging from white to red, which appear to cascade like fountains from rounded mounds of usually green foliage. Being warm-season, they are fast growing and enthusiastically produce longlasting flowers over an extended period—making them extremely valuable garden plants for use en masse or as individual specimens.

The diverse fountain grasses are mostly perennial, and largely clumping though several have a spreading habit. Many will set seed easily, causing some such as *Pennisetum setaceum* to be considered weeds in sensitive warmer areas. Coming

Panicum virgatum 'Warrior'. Photograph courtesy of Dianna Jazwinski.

Paspalum quadrifarium. Photograph courtesy of Dianna Jazwinski.

from warm to tropical climates, many will not survive temperate winters, and those that do require full sun and well-drained soils to perform well, though some light shade may be tolerated by hardier forms in areas of high sunlight. Some tropical species can be grown as summer annuals, including the dark-leaved and dark poker-like-flowered *Pennisetum glaucum* 'Purple Majesty'. Of the hardier forms, many have been chosen for their combination of flower and winter hardiness. Widely distributed in warm temperate to tropical areas.

'Fairy Tails'. Foxtail grass is a seedling selection from John Greenlee and one of the most striking and distinctive of fountain grasses, with light green mounds of leaves and masses of strongly upright dainty flowers, pinky white before quickly fading to tan, produced in profusion and over a long

Pennisetum 'Fairy Tails'. Photograph courtesy of Dianna Jazwinski.

period. A valuable addition to gardens where it can be used in large airy drifts, in groups at the front of the plant border and as informal hedges. Always prefers sun and open conditions. Apparently sterile. To 1.2 m (4 ft.). Z7–8.

'Paul's Giant'. A particularly distinctive form selected in the United States for its large, relatively tall spikes of fluffy creamy white flowers with good yellow-orange autumn foliage. To 1.5 m (5 ft.). Z6–7.

Pennisetum ×advena

syn *Pennisetum setaceum*
PURPLE FOUNTAIN GRASS
Until recently thought to be part of *Pennisetum setaceum*, these plants now have their own name as they are in fact somewhat different from that species (though *P. setaceum* is likely a parent). Not hardy except in very warm areas, most are effectively sterile so need to be increased by division from overwintered plants. Excellent pot subjects in colder areas. From Africa. Z9.

'Eaton Canyon'. A compact form with less vigour and purple leaf colour than its popular counterpart 'Rubrum'. To 75 cm ($2\frac{1}{2}$ ft.).

'Rubrum' ('Cupreum', 'Purpureum'). Absolutely stunning in colour, shape and form, this virtually unique grass has deep red to burgundy stems, foliage and exquisite red, very tactile arching flowers that gradually fade to beige with age. A perfect summer specimen, which will remain evergreen and flower year-round if given enough winter heat. Prefers a sunny spot with heat. To 1.2 m (4 ft.).

Pennisetum alopecuroides

syn *Pennisetum compressum, Pennisetum japonicum*
FOUNTAIN GRASS, FOXTAIL GRASS
This classic fountain grass has given rise to a whole series of cultivars with the same generally rounded mounds of green foliage, often colouring

golden yellow to mark the arrival of autumn, topped with a wealth of large fluffy bottlebrush-like flowers held on slightly arching stems. Relatively hardy in colder areas if given good drainage and a sunny open position. The species does not always flower reliably in such areas, though the cultivars do not appear to have the same shortcoming. In warmer to dry climates, fountain grasses may need more moisture and tolerate some light shade though they are always happy in full sun. Seed will set freely in warmer areas but does not appear to do so in colder places. From Asia. To 1.2 m (4 ft.). Z6–7.

'Cassian'. Produces dusky light brown flowers from midsummer onwards and turns rich orange-yellow in autumn. Named by Kurt Bluemel for well-known horticulturist Cassian Schmidt. To 90 cm (3 ft.).

'Caudatum'. Beautiful, with many large near-white fluffy flowers set above deep green foliage during summer. To 1.2 m (4 ft.).

'Dark Desire'. A new selection from Knoll Gardens with the most amazing, very large, dark purplish black bottlebrushes freely produced above bright green wide foliage. To 90 cm (3 ft.).

'Hameln'. A superb rounded compact form with very dark green wiry foliage and many fuzzy catkin-like flowers—which are not the largest, but are very freely produced and among the most reliable for cooler climates. To 90 cm (3 ft.).

'Herbstzauber'. A very attractive free-flowering selection with large fluffy greenish white flowers from high summer onwards, and bright green foliage. To 1.2 m (4 ft.).

'Little Bunny'. A miniature selection from 'Hameln', with small mounds of foliage and flower, more shyly produced in cooler climates. To 45 cm ($1\frac{1}{2}$ ft.).

'Little Honey'. A sport from 'Little Bunny', with the same characteristics except that leaves are

Pennisetum alopecuroides 'Cassian'

Pennisetum alopecuroides 'Dark Desire'.
Photograph courtesy of Dianna Jazwinski.

finely variegated with white and green stripes. To 45 cm (1½ ft.).

'Moudry'. A compact form with relatively wide, glossy, neat basal mounds of foliage topped by fluffy deep purple to black flowers held only just above leaf height. Later-flowering, to the point of non-flowering, in shorter summer areas. To 75 cm (2½ ft.).

'National Arboretum'. Very similar to 'Moudry' though flowers are held further above the dark green leaves. To 75 cm (2½ ft.).

'Red Head'. An excellent cultivar chosen for its early-flowering ability and relatively large individual flowers which open distinctly red before fading through purple shades to beige. To 90 cm (3 ft.).

'Viridescens' (var. *viridescens*). Considered a botanical variety by some, with strongly mound-forming glossy wide green leaves and a shy flowering habit in cooler areas. To 75 cm (2½ ft.).

'Weserbergland'. Lovely, with mounds of narrow green foliage and many creamy white flowers in late summer. To 90 cm (3 ft.).

'Woodside'. Selected in the U.K. for its habit of regular flowering, and similar to 'Hameln'

in many respects, 'Woodside' forms compact mounds of green foliage topped by many beige-white fluffy flowerheads from high summer onwards. To 90 cm (3 ft.).

Pennisetum incomptum

syn Pennisetum flaccidum

FOUNTAIN GRASS, FOXTAIL GRASS

A relatively hardy species, with narrow grey-green leaves and slender, daintily poised freely produced flowers. Its strongly spreading root system can be invasive and difficult to eradicate, demanding caution when used in any but the toughest and most contained areas. Prefers sun and is not fussy about soil. To 1.2 m (4 ft.). From China and Himalaya. Z4.

Pennisetum macrourum

FOUNTAIN GRASS, FOXTAIL GRASS

Forms spreading individual mounds of tough grey-green foliage with many distinct arching stems topped with rounded off-white flowerheads in summer. Very distinctive in full flower, though can be comparatively late to flower in cooler areas. Needs sun and a well- drained position. Variable from seed. From Africa. To 1.8 m (6 ft.). Z7.

'Short Stuff'. A selection from Knoll Gardens rather more compact and earlier to flower than the type, with freely produced flowers held just clear of the foliage. To 90 cm (3 ft.).

Pennisetum massaicum

FOUNTAIN GRASS, FOXTAIL GRASS

Coming from open savannah, this species is remarkably cold tolerant given its native range. Always prefers sun and well-drained conditions, and appears quite tolerant of heaver soils. Comes easily from seed and is usually represented by the following cultivar which itself comes fairly true from seed. From Africa. Z8.

Pennisetum alopecuroides 'Red Head'

'Red Buttons'. Bold, bright green mounds of gradually increasing foliage provide the base for enthusiastically produced, relatively short rounded flowers that are initially bright red before fading to tan and brown. Much earlier-flowering than most other fountain grasses; blooms can be almost continually produced on better soils. To 90 cm (3 ft.).

Pennisetum orientale
ORIENTAL FOUNTAIN GRASS

Less robust in growth and cold-hardiness than *Pennisetum alopecuroides*, with mounds of relatively narrow bright green to grey foliage and masses of soft pink (fading white) flowers freely produced from summer onwards. Clump-forming and best in full sun and well-drained soils. From Africa, Asia and India. To 60 cm (2 ft.). Z6.

'Karley Rose'. Forms mounds of shiny arching leaves and very deep rose pink flowers held on rather tall upright stems. Good in large drifts and masses and against more solid companions. To 1.2 m (4 ft.).

'Shogun'. Has more upright soft blush-pink

Pennisetum orientale 'Shogun'

Pennisetum massaicum 'Red Buttons'

Pennisetum orientale 'Tall Tails', emerging.
Photograph courtesy of Dianna Jazwinski.

flowers freely produced from high summer onwards, and distinct glaucous blue foliage. To 1.2 m (4 ft.).

'Tall Tails'. With light green mounds of foliage and many tall flowerheads with long, semi-pendulous white foxtail-like flowers. Can self-sow in warmer areas and is shorter-lived in colder districts. To 1.5 m (5 ft.).

Pennisetum setaceum

syn *Pennisetum ruppelii*

TENDER FOUNTAIN GRASS

Often grown as an annual in colder areas where it makes a highly ornamental plant in gardens. Contrastingly, its tendency to re-seed prolifically in warmer climates has led to invasiveness and it is considered a weed in areas such as mediterranean California. Prefers sun and well-drained soils, and goes summer-dormant in dry climates. From Africa and Asia. To 1.2 m (4 ft.). Z9.

Pennisetum villosum

FEATHERTOP

A firm garden favourite, with bright green, gradually spreading mounds of foliage covered with large, furry caterpillar-like fluffy white flowers. Tender in colder areas, where it can be grown as an annual, and reasonably hardy if given full sun and excellent drainage. From Africa. To 75 cm ($2\frac{1}{2}$ ft.). Z8.

Phalaris

CANARY GRASS

This group of widespread annual and perennial cool-season semi-evergreen grasses includes *Phalaris canariensis*, an annual often found in bird seed mixes.

Phalaris arundinacea

REED CANARY GRASS

A strongly spreading species found in moist areas and marshes, but avoiding open water, where it is

Pennisetum setaceum. Photograph courtesy of Rick Darke.

Pennisetum villosum

extremely vigorous and can cover very large areas. Excellent for restoration and conservation work in places where it is native. Only the variegated selections are usually found in gardens. All have running rootstocks that will eventually make large patches. From North America and Eurasia. To 1.5 m (5 ft.). Z4.

var. *picta* 'Arctic Sun'. A relatively new selection, with strongly marked creamy yellow to golden variegated foliage. More compact and less inclined to move around than the species. Prefers average to damp soils in sun or light shade. To 75 cm ($2\frac{1}{2}$ ft.).

var. *picta* 'Feesey' ('Strawberries and Cream'). Bright white-and-green-striped leaves occasionally suffused pinky red make this the boldest variegated form of *Phalaris arundinaceae*. Selected by noted grass specialist Mervyn Feesey. To 90 cm (3 ft.).

var. *picta* 'Luteopicta'. Seldom seen, with creamy yellow-striped foliage. Has less vigour than the species, and fades to white as the season progresses. To 75 cm ($2\frac{1}{2}$ ft.).

var. *picta* 'Picta'. Possibly the oldest known and most vigorous selection, often seen as large established patches in gardens. Bright white-and-green-striped leaves are sometimes suffused pink in cooler periods. To 1.2 m (4 ft.).

Phragmites

REED

Consisting of one species, this warm-season deciduous grass is widespread over most continents where it occurs in moist areas. Highly variable over its range.

Phragmites australis

COMMON REED

Has a vigorous questing rootstock that allows it to colonize a variety of wet and marshy areas,

Phalaris arundinacea var. *picta* 'Arctic Sun'

Phragmites australis. Photograph courtesy of Dianna Jazwinski.

gradually spreading to encompass vast tracts of land. Tough leaves are distinctively tapered in many shades of glaucous green. Of enormous benefit to biodiversity, it is much used for restoration and conservation projects. Prefers generally open areas. Widespread and common. To 4 m (13 ft.). Z4.

subsp. *australis* 'Variegatus'. Attractive with bright yellow-and-green-striped foliage, with considerable vigour and spreading ability. Happy in sun or light shade. To 2.7 m (9 ft.).

Poa

BLUE GRASS

Poa is a huge group of more than five hundred annual and perennial cool-season semi-evergreen grasses. Many are used as turf grass and in lawns; fine-textured, they resemble their close relatives, the fescues. Widespread in cool temperate regions.

Poa labillardierei. Photograph courtesy of Dianna Jazwinski.

Poa labillardierei

AUSTRALIAN BLUE GRASS

During summer, with enough moisture, large mounds of steely blue narrow foliage and a succession of silvery blue stems and flowers are continually produced from the centre. In full flower this poa is a shimmering haze of silvery blue. Happiest in sun or very light shade. Prefers dry soils in colder areas, and more moisture in warmer climates. From Australia. To 1.2 m (4 ft.). Z8.

Rhynchospora

WHITE-TOP SEDGE, STAR SEDGE

These mostly perennial, evergreen grass-like sedges prefer moist soils with some degree of sun. Their distinctive flowers are in fact extended bracts. Widespread in warm temperate regions.

Rhynchospora latifolia

syn *Dichromena latifolia*

STAR SEDGE

Native to pond edges, swamps and savannahs, with conspicuously elongated white bracts held on thin green stems. Happy in a variety of damp areas. Increases by a slowly running rootstock. From the U.S. To 75 cm ($2\frac{1}{2}$ ft.). Z8.

Saccharum

SUGAR CANE

This group of several dozen warm-season deciduous grass species is best known for the commercial production of sugar cane from *Saccharum officinarum*, which can also be a very attractive ornamental plant in its own right. Sugar canes have some broad similarities to miscanthus, with which they can be mistaken in gardens especially when not in flower, as they form similar large mounds of wide green leaves—though these are topped with plumes that give them a superficial resemblance to pampas. Previously a separate genus, *Erianthus* is now included under *Saccharum*. Sugar canes prefer open moist situations to fuel their fast rate of growth, though they seem happy enough adapting to drier areas in gardens. Widely distributed in temperate to tropical areas.

Saccharum arundinaceum
HARDY SUGAR CANE

Fast-growing and variable from seed, the best forms having rather attractive, wide, almost-glaucous sea green foliage that can make very large mounds. Stiff upright plumes, produced in late summer, are initially a wonderful deep pinky red before fading to silver-grey. Happiest in full sun in a range of soils. Excellent as a specimen plant or to provide screening and division. From Asia. To 4 m (14 ft.). Z7.

Saccharum officinarum
SUGAR CANE

Well-known for its provision of cane sugar. Can attain massive proportions of up to 6 m (20 ft.) high in tropical areas, where it is valued for its ornamental qualities. In less favoured localities it is often used as a tender or seasonal subject where it is less vigorous. Forms with purple-tinted foliage are especially favoured in gardens. Prefers sunny open positions with sufficient moisture, but is at least seasonally drought tolerant. From Asia. To 2.4 m (8 ft.). Z10.

'Pele's Smoke'. A beautiful form with dramatically marked dark purplish black stems and lighter reddish purple-tinted foliage. Very ornamental, with less vigour than the green forms. Always best in sun and reasonable soils. To 2.1 m (7 ft.).

Saccharum ravennae
syn *Erianthus ravennae*
RAVENNA GRASS

Clump-forming, with large mounds of grey-green

Rhynchospora latifolia. Photograph courtesy of Dianna Jazwinski.

Saccharum ravennae

leaves which support masses of tightly packed, tall, sometimes-arching upright stems and pampas-like flower plumes of a delicate silvery pink, fading to silver-grey. Requires a long season to bloom well, so is best in full sun in a variety of soils. From Africa, Asia and Europe. To 3 m (10 ft.). Z6.

Schizachyrium

BLUESTEM, BEARDGRASS

Among this large group of widely distributed annual and perennial warm-season deciduous grasses, only *S. scoparium* is readily cultivated in gardens. Until relatively recently, this species was classified under the genus *Andropogon*, from which it differs due to the structure of its flowers. Widely distributed in temperate to tropical areas.

Schizachyrium scoparium

Schizachyrium scoparium

syn *Andropogon scoparium*

LITTLE BLUESTEM

Beautiful, tough and adaptable, little bluestem is a major constituent of the American tall grass prairie. Usually clumping, with basal mounds of fine-textured leaves and characteristically upright to strongly vertical stems. Flowers offer a striking palette of reds, oranges, coppers and rust in autumn. Foliage and stems are often glaucous to silvery blue and several selections have been made for this quality. Others have been selected for use as forage grass but some such as 'Aldous' and 'Blaze' have valuable ornamental qualities as well. Always best in full open sun but occasionally tolerates light shade. Does well in a range of soils from wet to fairly dry; poor rather than fertile soils will produce the most upright growth. Extremely variable from seed. From North America. To 1.2 m (4 ft.). Z3–8.

'Prairie Blues'. A seed-raised strain, with a generally upright habit and stems and leaves of an overall grey-green appearance, turning warm orange and brown in autumn. Needs full sun and well-drained poor soil for best growth.

'Stars and Stripes'. Chosen for its creamy yellow-and-green-striped basal mounds of foliage. To 90 cm (3 ft.).

'The Blues'. An excellent selection by Kurt Bluemel with striking glaucous blue stems and a sturdy habit.

Schoenoplectus

CLUBRUSH

Also known as bulrush, causing some confusion with *Typha* species which have the same common name, the clubrushes are annual and perennial semi-evergreen grass-like sedges, found in a wide range of aquatic or waterside situations. Forming large colonies of dark green to glaucous grey rounded stems, they are a key ingredient of wetland areas where they are valuable as cover for wildlife and for the filtering capacity of their dense root systems. Many of the formerly separate *Scirpus* species are now included in this group. Clubrushes have been used for traditional thatching and matting purposes in several different cultures. Widely distributed in temperate areas.

Schoenoplectus californicus

syn *Scirpus californicus*

CALIFORNIA BULRUSH, GIANT BULRUSH, TULE

Has a rapidly growing habit, producing tall cylindrical grey-green stems with interesting brown flowers at the very tips. Can cover large areas and is always best in full sun and boggy soils or marshes. From the southern U.S. through Argentina. To 2.7 m (9 ft.). Z7.

Schoenoplectus lacustris subsp. *tabernaemontani*

syn *Schoenoplectus lacustris*, *Scirpus tabernaemontani*

COMMON CLUB RUSH

Commonplace in most temperate areas in a wide variety of wet situations, from the open water of lakes and ponds to brackish marshes—anywhere with sufficient moisture. A spreading root system allows it to thrive in such marginal conditions, creating large clumps of generally upright dark green to occasionally grey rounded stems that will eventually cover significant ground. This widely established variable species inevitably has a complex mix of very similar forms, leading to conflicting botanical treatments and naming. However named, plants in this group are key to wetland and restoration schemes and effective in larger water garden areas. Best in sun and tolerant of most levels of moisture. To 2.1 m (7 ft.). Z4.

'Albescens' ('Variegatus'). Effectively clump-forming, with very upright narrow stems vertically striped light green and white. Ideal for the pond's edge or as a specimen in small artificial water features. To 1.5 m (5 ft.).

'Zebrinus'. With narrow upright stems, dark green with vivid light yellow horizontal banding. Ideal for the pond's edge or as a specimen. To 1.2 m (4 ft.).

Sesleria

MOOR GRASS

This modest group of sturdy often-evergreen cool-season clump-forming grasses offer some extremely gardenworthy choices that work well in various situations, as ground cover or in drifts, meadows or living roofs. Coming from dry, rocky

Schoenoplectus lacustris subsp. *tabernaemontani* 'Albescens'

places, they are very adaptable and tolerate a range of soils as well as partial shade, though they are happiest in sun.

'Greenlee's Hybrid'. A most interesting cultivated selection, assumed to be a hybrid between *S. autumnalis* and *S. caerulea*, exhibiting characteristics from both presumed parents. Hardy, with improved tolerance to high inland temperatures, happy in sun or partial shade. To 20 cm (8 in.). Z4.

Sesleria autumnalis

AUTUMN MOOR GRASS

Strong mounds of yellowish, almost chartreuse, usually evergreen foliage mark this tough and adaptable plant apart from other more blue-foliaged species. Freely produced, relatively insignificant creamy white flowers contribute to the overall effect. Happy in full sun or light shade in a variety of soils. Excellent for meadows, drifts and roof gardens. From southern Europe. To 45 cm ($1\frac{1}{2}$ ft.). Z4.

Sesleria caerulea

syn *Sesleria albicans*

BLUE MOOR GRASS

A much-underused, tightly mound-forming evergreen species grown primarily for its distinctive foliage, light glaucous blue on the upper surface and darker green below. Leaves are held so that both colours are visible at the same time, though the overall effect is blue. Dark at first, pale spikes of flowers are produced on short stems early in the season. Superb as ground cover, for meadows and for green roofs where it seldom needs trimming. Drought-tolerant in sun or light shade. From Europe and the U.K. To 20 cm (8 in.). Z4.

Sesleria heufleriana

BLUE-GREEN MOOR GRASS

Similar in many respects to blue moor grass, but with taller flowers and broader tufted mounds, coloured slightly more grey-green. Happy in sun or light shade in a variety of different soils. From Europe. To 40 cm (16 in.). Z4.

Sesleria nitida

GREY MOOR GRASS

An Italian species, forming mounds of spiky blue-grey leaves topped by attractive light flowerheads held clear above the foliage on slightly pendulous stems in late spring. Prefers a sunny open spot and is reasonably drought tolerant. From Europe. To 60 cm (2 ft.). Z4.

Setaria

FOXTAIL GRASS

This reasonably large group of annual and perennial warm-season evergreen grasses is often weedy in nature; only a few are consciously cultivated. Widely distributed in tropical to temperate areas.

Setaria macrostachya

BRISTLE GRASS

A very pretty annual grass that finds use in cool temperate gardens. Wide light green leaves are topped by many rounded flowerheads during summer, the whole plant assuming red tints as the season progresses. Will self-seed if happy. Prefers a sunny open spot. From Asia. To 45 cm ($1\frac{1}{2}$ ft.). Z9.

Setaria palmifolia

PALM GRASS

A striking tropical non-hardy grass with large, wide, rich green leaves, conspicuously pleated and often red-tinted. Tall narrow purplish inflorescences appear in late summer. Used in seasonal displays and as a summer pot specimen in colder areas. Re-seeds in warmer climates. Best in a sunny spot where not too dry. From Asia. To 1.2 m (4 ft.). in cultivation. Z9.

Sesleria autumnalis

Sesleria caerulea

Setaria macrostachya. Photograph courtesy of Dianna Jazwinski.

Sorghastrum

INDIAN GRASS

Though only *S. nutans* is commonly cultivated, this group includes both annual and perennial species of warm-season evergreen grasses. From Africa and North America. Z3–6.

Sorghastrum nutans

syn *Sorghastrum avenaceum*

INDIAN GRASS

Once extremely common in tall grass prairie, this beautiful, adaptable, mostly clump-forming species contributes strongly upright flower stems from mounds of often-glaucous blue leaves. Changing colour in tune with the seasons and variable from seed, it has given rise to several notable selections, all best in full sun and with adequate moisture. From North America, including Mexico. To 2.4 m (8 ft.). Z3.

'Bluebird'. A good glaucous-leaved selection from the Bluebird Nursery in Clarkson, Nebraska. To 1.5 m (5 ft.).

'Indian Steel'. An excellent form with, as its name suggests, steel grey foliage and an upright habit. To 1.5 m (5 ft.).

'Müllerslust'. An upright habit and very glaucous grey leaves distinguish this German selection. To 1.5 m (5 ft.).

'Sioux Blue'. A first-class selection from Rick Darke, with very blue-grey leaves and stems and an upright nature. To 1.5 m (5 ft.).

Spartina

CORD GRASS

These primarily coastal, perennial, warm-season evergreen grasses prefer wet soils to brackish and saltwater environments and are of major importance to coastal ecologies where they are used in restoration and habitat provision. Vigorous spreading root systems can preclude their use in all but the largest of gardens.

Spartina pectinata

PRAIRIE CORD GRASS

Found in freshwater habitats to wet prairie lands throughout much of North America, prairie cord grass will grow happily in most soils, even tolerating seasonal droughts, which makes it amenable to garden situations. Strongly spreading, it can form dense patches of strong bright green foliage and relatively lightweight panicles of flower that can weigh down the narrow stems as the season progresses. Best in open sunny conditions with

Spartina pectinata 'Aureomarginata'.
Photograph courtesy of Dianna Jazwinski.

some moisture. From North America. To 2.1 m (7 ft.). Z3.

'Aureomarginata' ('Variegata'). Bold, bright yellow-and-green-striped foliage on slightly less vigorous plants make this a good selection for gardens. To 2.1 m (7 ft.).

Spodiopogon

GREYBEARD GRASS

Among this small group of perennial warm-season deciduous species at home in open grassland, only one species is cultivated to any extent.

Spodiopogon sibiricus

SIBERIAN GREYBEARD GRASS

A distinctive grass with a neatly rounded form. Thin green flat leaves, held nearly horizontal, turn a wonderful deep red in most autumns. Erect terminal panicles emerge in late summer. Best in light shade where not too dry; tolerates even more shade, although its form will not be as tight. From China, Japan and Siberia. To 1.2 m (4 ft.). Z3.

'West Lake'. Collected from China, this form introduced by Roy Lancaster and Hans Simon has noticeably pinkish red flowerheads. To 1.2 m (4 ft.).

Sporobolus

DROPSEED

This very large group of annual and perennial warm-season deciduous grasses is mostly represented in gardens by the temperate North American species that are found in mostly open grasslands. From tropical to temperate areas.

Sporobolus airoides

ALKALI SACATON, ALKALI DROPSEED

Produces clumps of relatively coarse grey-green foliage topped with very graceful arching flowerheads, opening pink before fading to silver in late summer. Can colour an attractive yellow-orange in autumn. Well-adapted to alkaline soils as well as a variety of testing conditions, including drought and heat where it may produce more compact growth. Always prefers sunny open positions. From the southern and western U.S. To 1.2 m (4 ft.). Z4.

Sporobolus heterolepis

PRAIRIE DROPSEED

Relatively slow-growing and refined, this is regarded as one of the most elegant of prairie grasses, forming finely textured dense flowing mounds that turn deep orange to copper in

Sporobolus heterolepis

winter. Delicate flower panicles sit high above the foliage on slender stalks, with fresh flowers having a slight fragrance redolent of coriander. Long-lived and very drought-tolerant. A good choice for meadow, prairie and ground cover plantings. Prefers full sun but tolerates light shade in a variety of different soils. From North America. To 75 cm (2½ ft.). Z3.

'Tara'. A compact selection from Roy Diblik, with slightly stiffer foliage and good orange-red autumn colour. To 60 cm (2 ft.).

'Wisconsin'. Selected by Hans Simon for reliable flowering under cooler European conditions.

Sporobolus wrightii

GIANT SACATON

The largest of all dropseeds, with grey-green clumps of arching foliage topped by sculptural

Sporobolus wrightii

flower spikes that offer dramatic impact over a long period. Amazingly drought-tolerant and even shows some resistance to salt in coastal situations. Always best in sun. From the southern U.S. to Mexico. To 2.4 m (8 ft.). Z5.

Stipa

FEATHER GRASS, NEEDLE GRASS

This large group of mostly clump-forming cool-season evergreen grasses, originating in Africa and Eurasia, have long been used extensively in gardens. From Africa and Eurasia.

THE SPLITTING OF STIPA

Recent taxonomic research has led to several grasses previously well-known as stipas being reclassified under other genera. Although perhaps irritating to gardeners uninterested in the background science, the name changes have been observed here purely for expediency as the new names are already in general circulation.

Stipa arundinacea: see *Anemanthele lessoniana* (page 172), *Stipa calamagrostis*: see *Achnatherum calamagrostis* (page 168), *Stipa coronata*: see *Achnatherum coronatum* (page 168), *Stipa elegantissima*: see *Austrostipa elegantissima* (page 175), *Stipa extremiorientalis*: see *Achnatherum extremiorientale* (page 169), *Stipa ichu*: see *Jarava ichu* (page 208), *Stipa ramosissima*: see *Austrostipa ramosissima* (page 175), *Stipa tenuissima*: see *Nassella tenuissima* (page 228).

Stipa barbata

FEATHER GRASS

From tidy clumps of rather uninteresting green foliage appear magnificent, slender, arching silvery flowerheads with a flowing motion even in the slightest of breezes. Requires a sunny well-drained spot. Can be difficult to establish. From southern Europe and northern Africa. To 75 cm ($2\frac{1}{2}$ ft.). Z7.

Stipa gigantea

GIANT OAT GRASS, SPANISH OAT GRASS

The largest and most striking of all stipas. Tough narrow green foliage eventually forms significantly sized basal clumps from which come the most amazing tall heads of light golden brown to buff oat-like flowers, with an airy see-through quality despite their size and number. Produced early in the season, stems and flowers last for many months. Unsurpassed as a mature specimen, it must have full sun and is best in a well-drained spot. Variable from seed, which is not viable in colder areas. Dislikes being shaded or having other plants too close. From southern Europe and northern Africa. To 2.4 m (8 ft.). Z5.

'Gold Fontaene'. A spectacular selection by German nurseryman Ernst Pagels. Huge clumps of narrow foliage and many stiff spikes of enormous golden brown upright flowerheads held high above the foliage make this the perfect form of Spanish oat grass.

'Pixie'. A comparatively dwarf selection with

Stipa gigantea 'Gold Fontaene'

less vigour than the species—but with all of its airy gracefulness, and just as useful. To 1.5 m (5 ft.).

Stipa pennata
EUROPEAN FEATHER GRASS
Flowerheads bearing long, feathery tails are held well above tight clumps of slightly arching leaves. Can be difficult to establish and must have a sunny well-drained spot. Often confused with *S. barbata*. From Europe, Africa and Asia. To 75 cm ($2\frac{1}{2}$ ft.). Z6.

Stipa gigantea 'Pixie'

Stipa pulcherrima
EUROPEAN FEATHER GRASS
Similar to *S. barbata* and *S. pennata* and equally graceful, with even longer flowering tails produced from mounds of ordinary green leaves. Needs full sun. From Europe, Africa and Asia. To 75 cm ($2\frac{1}{2}$ ft.). Z6.

Tridens
This small group of warm-season deciduous perennial grasses originates in areas ranging from woodland edge to open meadow in the eastern United States through Mexico.

Tridens flavus
PURPLETOP
Upright and clump-forming, providing distinct hues of purple in meadows, woodland edges and open grasslands during summer when the graceful flowers are freshly opened. Prefers sun but will tolerate some light shade in a variety of soils, ideally with some moisture. From the eastern U.S. through Mexico. To 1.2 m (4 ft.). Z6.

Typha
BULRUSH, CATTAIL, REEDMACE
The deciduous, grass-like cattails are present in most areas, in any suitable moist to wet ground but especially common along drainage ditches and on streamsides and riverbanks. Tolerating saline and partially polluted waters, they are essential to wetland ecology, providing habitat for wildlife and acting as a natural filtering system. Widely distributed in temperate and tropical areas.

Typha angustifolia
LESSER BULRUSH, NARROW-LEAVED CATTAIL
A more slender and refined version of *T. latifolia*, with many spikes of distinctive rounded brown

flowerheads, separated into male and female parts by a small gap on the flower stem. Has a spreading habit and will colonize large areas under suitable conditions. From North and South America and Eurasia. To 1.8 m (6 ft.). Z3.

Typha latifolia
COMMON BULRUSH, COMMON CATTAIL, GREAT REEDMACE

The most common *Typha* species, found in any suitably wet area. Forms vigorous spreading clumps of tall upright foliage and rounded cylindrical brown flowerheads that are not separated like those of the narrow-leaved cattail. Will cover large areas though always prefers sunny open positions. Widely distributed in the northern hemisphere, South America and Africa. To 2.7 m (9 ft.). Z3.

'Variegata'. A striking variegated form, with very attractive bright creamy white and green variegated foliage and typical bulrush flowers. Ideal in containers but less cold-hardy than the species. To 1.5 m (5 ft.).

Tridens flavus

Typha minima
MINIATURE CATTAIL

A distinctive miniature form, smaller than other cattails in all its parts with the same running habit, bright green leaves and narrowly pointed male and oval female flowers separated by a section of bare stem. Will tolerate the water's edge or very moist soils in sun or lightest shade. Perfect for small watery areas. From Eurasia. To 75 cm ($2\frac{1}{2}$ ft.). Z5.

Uncinia
HOOK SEDGE

The grass-like hook sedges produce seeds that hook themselves onto passing animals, including gardeners, for distribution. Although this group of perennial, mostly clump-forming evergreens is relatively large, only a few are used in gardens. From Australasia and South America. Z8.

Uncinia rubra
HOOK SEDGE

Unassuming tussocks of deep reddish brown evergreen foliage produce tiny insignificant flowers that eventually turn into hooked seeds. Often confused with two similar species, *U. egmontiana* and *U. unciniata*, from which it differs due to its more compact nature and narrower, more uniform darker purplish to bronze-red foliage. Prefers sun for best colour, and not-too-dry soil. From New Zealand. To 30 cm (1 ft.). Z8.

'Everflame'. A recent, very attractive selection, with reddish brown leaves striped with shades of pink.

Typha latifolia

Uncinia rubra

Uncinia rubra 'Everflame'

HARDINESS ZONES

The Hardiness Zone ratings that appear through the Directory of Grasses and Grass-like Plants refer to the minimum temperatures at which a given plant is likely to be able to thrive. If you know the minimum temperature of your area, the chart below will give the corresponding Zone.

Local climatic conditions can and do vary enormously, even within a small area, and cultural conditions exert a strong influence on a plant's tolerance of a temperature range. Zone information can therefore only serve as a very general guideline as to whether a plant is likely to do well in your garden.

MINIMUM TEMPERATURE (CELSIUS)	ZONE	MINIMUM TEMPERATURE (FAHRENHEIT)
below −45	1	below −50
−45 to −40	2	−50 to −40
−40 to −34	3	−40 to −30
−34 to −29	4	−30 to −20
−29 to −23	5	−20 to −10
−23 to −18	6	−10 to 0
−18 to −12	7	0 to 10
−12 to −7	8	10 to 20
−7 to −1	9	20 to 30
−1 to 4	10	30 to 40
above 4	11	above 40

WHERE TO SEE GRASSES

This list represents only a tiny fraction of the many gardens and designed spaces that have used grasses successfully. As grasses increase in popularity, more and more public spaces, parks, shopping centres and commercial operations will also have successful schemes from which to gain inspiration.

UNITED STATES

The Battery Promenade and the Gardens of Remembrance, New York, New York. www.thebattery.org

Chanticleer Garden, 786 Church Road, Wayne, Pennsylvania 19087. www.chanticleergarden.org

Chicago Botanic Garden, 1000 Lake Cook Road, Glencoe, Illinois 60022. www.chicago-botanic.org

The High Line, New York, New York. www.thehighline.org

Huntington Botanical Gardens, 1151 Oxford Road, San Marino, California 91108. www.huntington.org

Leaning Pine Arboretum, Calpoly State University, San Luis Obispo, California 93407. www.leaningpinearboretum.calpoly.edu

Longwood Gardens, US Route 1, PO Box 501, Kennett Square, Pennsylvania 19348. www.longwoodgardens.org

Lurie Garden, Millennium Park, The Welcome Centre, 201 E.Randolph Street, Chicago, Illinois. www.millenniumpark.org

Mt. Cuba Center Inc, 3120 Barley Mill Road, Hockessin, Deleware 19707. www.mtcubacenter.org

Native Sons, Inc. 379 W. El Campo Road, Arroyo Grande, California 93420. www.nativeson.com

Rancho Santa Ana Botanic Garden, 1500 North College Avenue, Claremont, California 91711. www.rsabg.org

Regional Parks Botanic Garden, Wildcat Canyon Road, c/o Tilden Regional Park, Berkeley, California 94708-2396. www.nativeplants.org www.ebparks.org

San Diego Zoo's Wild Animal Park, 15500 San Pasqual Valley Road, Escondido, California 92027-7017. www.sandiegozoo.org

San Francisco Botanical Garden at Strybing Arboretum, Ninth Avenue at Lincoln Way, San Francisco, California 94122. www.sfbotanicalgarden.org

The Santa Barbara Botanic Garden, 1212 Mission Canyon Road, Santa Barbara, California 93105. www.sbbg.org

The Scott Arboretum of Swarthmore College, 500 College Avenue, Swarthmore, Pennsylvania 19081. www.scottarboretum.org

Springs Preserve, 333 S.Valley View Blvd, between US 95 and Alta Drive, Las Vegas, Nevada. www.springspreserve.org

UNITED KINGDOM

Beth Chatto Gardens, Elmstead Market, Colchester, CO7 7DB. www.bethchatto.co.uk

Blooms of Bressingham, Bressingham, Diss, Norfolk, IP22 2AB. www.bloomsofbressingham.co.uk

Cambo House, Kingsbarn, St Andrews, Fife, KY16 8QD. www.camboestate.com

Knoll Gardens, Hampreston, Wimborne, Dorset, BH21 7ND. www.knollgardens.co.uk

Lady Farm Gardens, Lady Farm, Chelwood, Somerset, BS39 4NN. www.ladyfarm.com

Pensthorpe, Fakenham Road, Fakenham, Norfolk, NR21 0LN. www.pensthorpe.com

The Royal Botanic Gardens Kew, Richmond, Surrey, TW9 3AE. www.kew.org

The RHS Garden Harlow Carr, Crag Lane, Harrogate, North Yorkshire, HG3 1QB. www.rhs.org.uk

The RHS Garden Hyde Hall, Buckhatch Lane, Rettendon, Chelmsford, Essex CM3 8ET. www.rhs.org.uk

The RHS Garden Rosemoor, Great Torrington, Devon, EX38 8PH. www.rhs.org.uk

The RHS Garden Wisley, Wisley, Woking, Surrey, GU23 6QB. www.rhs.org.uk

Scampston Hall, Malton, North Yorkshire, YO17 8NG. www.scampston.co.uk

Sir Harold Hillier Gardens, Jermyns Lane, Ampfield, Romsey, Hampshire, SO51 0QA. www.hilliergardens.org.uk

The Trentham Estate, Stone Road, Trentham, Stoke on Trent, ST4 8JG. www.trenthamleisure.co.uk

EUROPE

Berggarten Hannover, Herrenhäuser Str.4, 30419 Hannover, Germany. www.berggarten-hannover.de

Karl-Foerster-Garten, Am Raubfang 6, 14469 Potsdam-Bornim, Germany

Hermannshof, Babostrasse 5, D-69469 Weinheim/Bergstrasse, Germany. www.sichtungsgarten-hermannshof.de

Le Jardin Plume, 76116 Auzouville sur Ry, France. www.lejardinplume.com

Lehrgaerten Weihenstephan, Am Staudengarten 9, 85350 Freising, Munich, Germany. www.hswt.de

Oudolf Nursery, Broekstraat 17, 6999 DE Hummelo, Netherlands. www.oudolf.com

Overdam Nursery, Agiltevej 11, DK-2970 Hørsholm, Denmark. www.overdam.dk

Priona Gardens, Schuineslootweg 13, 7777 RE Schuinesloot, Netherlands. www.prionatuinen.com

Westpark, West Street, 80539 Munich, Germany

WHERE TO BUY GRASSES

This list represents only a tiny percentage of the nurseries and other outlets that sell grasses; there are, of course, many more wonderful outlets that are not listed here.

UNITED STATES

Berkeley Horticultural Nursery, 1310 McGee Avenue, Berkeley, California 94703. www.berkeleyhort.com

Daryll's Nursery, 15770 Ellendale Road, Dallas, Oregon 97338. www.daryllsnursery.com

Digging Dog Nursery, P.O. Box 471, Albion, California 95410. www.diggingdog.com

Earthly Pursuits Inc, 2901 Kuntz Rd, Windsor Mill, Maryland 21244. www.earthlypursuits.net

Granite Seed, 1697 W. 2100 North Lehi, Utah 84043. www.graniteseed.com

Greenlee Nursery Inc, 6075, C Kimball Avenue, Chino, California 91780. www.greenleenursery.com

High Country Gardens, 2902 Rufina Street, Santa Fe, New Mexico 87507. www.highcountrygardens.com

Hoffman Nursery, 5520 Bahama Road, Rougemont, North Carolina 27572. www.hoffmannursery.com

Jelitto Perennial Seeds (NA Office), 125 Chenoweth Lane, Suite 301, Louisville, Kentucky 40207. www.jelitto.com

Kurt Bluemel Inc, 2740 Greene Lane, Baldwin, Maryland 21013. www.kurtbluemel.com

Larner Seeds, P.O. Box 407, Bolinas, California 94924. www.larnerseeds.com

Mostly Native Nursery, P.O. Box 258, 27235 Highway One, Tomales, California 94971. www.mostlynatives.com

Mountain States Wholesale Nursery, P.O. Box 2500, Litchfield Park, Arizona 85340. www.mswn.com

The Native Plant Nursery, P.O. Box 7841, Ann Arbor, Michigan 48107. www.nativeplant.com

Native Sons Wholesale, 379 W. El Campo Road, Arroyo Grande, California 93420. www.nativeson.com

North Creek Nurseries Wholesale, R.R. 2, Box 33, Landenberg, Pennsylvania 19350. www.northcreeknurseries.com

Northwind Perennial Farm, 7047 Hospital Road, Burlington, Wisconsin 53105. www.northwindperennialfarm.com

Pinelands Nursery, 323 Island Road, Columbus, New Jersey 09022. www.pinelandsnursery.com

Plant Delights Nursery, 9241 Sauls Road, Raleigh, North Carolina 27603. www.plantdelights.com

Plants of the Southwest, Agua Fria, Route 6, Box 11A, Sante Fe, New Mexico 87501. www.plantsofthesouthwest.com

Steve Schmidt Nursery, P.O. Box 53, 29977 SE Weitz Lane, Eagle Creek, Oregon 97022. www.steveschmidtnursery.com

Stock Seed Farms, 28008 Mill Road, Murdock, Nebraska 68407. www.stockseed.com

Triple Oaks Nursery, P.O. Box 385, 2359 S. Delsea Drive, Franklinville, New Jersey 08322. www.tripleoaks.com

Walla Walla Nursery Co, 4176 Stateline Road, Walla Walla, Washington 99362 www.wallawallanursery.com.

Western Native Seed, P.O. Box 188, Coaldale, Colorado 81222. www.westernnativeseed.com

Wildtype Design, Native Plants and Seeds, 900 N. Every Road, Mason, Michigan 28854. www.wildtypeplants.com

Wind Poppy Farm and Nursery, 3171 Unick Road, Ferndale, Washington 98238. www.windpoppy.com

Wind River Seed, 3075 Lane 51½, Manderson, Wyoming 82432. www.windriverseed.com

CANADA

Bluestem Nursery, 16 Kingsley Road, Christina Lake, British Columbia, V0H 1E3. www.bluestem.ca

UNITED KINGDOM

The Alpine and Grass Nursery, Northgate, Pinchbeck, Spalding, Lincolnshire, PE11 3TB. www.alpineandgrasses.co.uk

Beth Chatto Gardens, Elmstead Market, Colchester, CO7 7DB. www.bethchatto.co.uk

The Big Grass Company, Hookhill Plantation, Woolfardisworthy East, Devon, EX17 4RX. www.big-grass.com

Blooms of Bressingham, Bressingham, Diss, Norfolk, IP22 2AB. www.bloomsofbressingham.co.uk

Eversley Nursery, 10 Granville Avenue, Hesketh Bank, Preston, Lancashire, PR4 6AH. www.eversleynursery.co.uk

Hoecroft Plants, Severals Grange, Holt Road, Wood Norton, Dereham, Norfolk, NR20 5BL. www.hoecroft.co.uk

Knoll Gardens, Hampreston, Wimborne, Dorset, BH21 7ND. www.knollgardens.co.uk

Marchants Hardy Plants, 2 Marchants Cottages, Mill Lane, Laughton, East Sussex, BN8 6AJ. www.marchantshardyplants.co.uk

Oak Tree Nursery, Mill Lane, Barlow, Selby, North Yorkshire, YO8 8EY. www.oaktreenursery.com

The Plantsman's Preference, Hopton Road, Garboldisham, Diss, Norfolk, IP22 2QN. www.plantpref.co.uk

The RHS Garden Harlow Carr, Crag Lane, Harrogate, North Yorkshire, HG3 1QB. www.rhs.org.uk

The RHS Garden Hyde Hall, Buckhatch Lane, Rettendon, Chelmsford, Essex CM3 8ET. www.rhs.org.uk

The RHS Garden Rosemoor, Great Torrington, Devon, EX38 8PH. www.rhs.org.uk

The RHS Garden Wisley, Wisley, Woking, Surrey, GU23 6QB. www.rhs.org.uk

Scampston Hall, Malton, North Yorkshire, YO17 8NG. www.scampston.co.uk

EUROPE

Bambous de Planbuisson, Rue Montaigne, 24480 Le Buisson de Cadouin, France. www.planbuisson.com

Le Jardin Plume, 76116 Auzouville sur Ry, France. www.lejardinplume.com

Oudolf Nursery, Broekstraat 17, 6999 DE Hummelo, Netherlands. www.oudolf.com

Overdam Nursery, Agiltevej 11, DK-2970 Hørsholm, Denmark. www.overdam.dk

Staudengärtner Klose, Rosenstrasse 10, D-34253 Lohfelden, Germany. www.staudengaertner-klose.de

PLANTING DISTANCES AND DENSITIES

The following chart gives suggestions for the number of plants that should be used per square metre or yard of planting area, for a wide range of grasses discussed in this book.

Thinking in terms of the number of plants per square metre or yard can be very useful in calculating (and re-calculating) the plants needed for the whole area. Simply multiple the number of plants needed per square metre or yard by the total number of metres or yards available to plant.

Numbers of plants needed have been given in a suggested range, which really depends on the size of plants used and the purpose for which they are being planted. For example, if a dense cover is required for ground cover, then the higher number is likely to be the best option. Contrastingly, if more space can be left between the plants, as in gravel plantings, then a lower number may be more appropriate. If smaller plants such as plugs are being used, perhaps for the relatively even surface of a lawn replacement, then you may need a higher density of the smaller plants is than is suggested here. Local climatic conditions also make a difference; in warmer areas of fast growth, the lower planting density may be sufficient, while in colder areas a higher plant density may be needed to provide the same cover.

To keep the area from looking patchy, try to use no more than one type of grass per square metre or yard. For instance, in a planting area of thirty square metres or yards, no more than thirty different grasses should be used. And ideally, allowing for repeated groups of the same plant, this number should be closer to around ten different plants covering three squares each, or even five plants covering six squares each.

Suggested number of plants per square metre or yard

Achnatherum, 1–3
Acorus, 7–9
Agrostis, 5–11
Alopecurus, 3–7
Ammophila, 3–9
Anemanthele, 1–3
Andropogon, 3–5
Ampeledesmos, 1–3
Aristida, 3–5
Arrhenatherum, 3–7
Arundo, 1–3
Austrostipa, 1–3
Baumea, 5–7
Bothriochloa, 3–5
Bouteloua, 3–5
Briza, 5–9
Bromus, 3–5
Calamagrostis, 1–3
Carex, smaller forms such as *C. flacca*, 7–11
Carex, medium forms such as *C. oshimensis* 'Evergold', 3–7
Carex, larger forms such as *C. pendula*, 1–3

Chasmanthium, 3–5
Chionochloa, 1–3
Cortaderia, 1–3
Cyperus, 1–3
Deschampsia, 5–7
Desmoschoenus, 3–5
Elymus, 3–5
Eragrostis, 3–5
Eriophorum, 5–7
Festuca, smaller forms such as *F. rubra* and *F. amethystina*, 5–9
Festuca, medium forms such as *F. californica*, 3–5
Festuca, larger forms such as *F. mairei*, 1–3
Glyceria, 1–3
Hakonechloa, 5–7
Helictotrichon, 3–5
Holcus, 3–7
Hordeum, 7–9
Imperata, 7–11
Jarava, 3–5
Juncus, 3–5

Koeleria, 5–7
Leymus, 1–5
Luzula, 5–7
Melica, 3–7
Melinis, 5–7
Milium, 5–7
Miscanthus, most full-sized forms, 1–3
Miscanthus, smaller forms such as *M. sinensis* 'Gold Bar', 'Little Kitten' and 'Little Zebra', 3–5
Molinia caerulea and its cultivars, 3–5
Molinia caerulea subsp. *arundinacea* and its cultivars, 1–3
Nassella, 3–5
Ophiopogon, most forms, 5–9
Ophiopogon, small-leaved forms such as *O. japonicus* 'Minor', 9–11

Oryzopsis, 3–5
Panicum, 1–5
Paspalum, 1–3
Pennisetum, 3–5
Phalaris, 3–5
Phragmites, 1–3
Poa, 1–5
Rhynchopsora, 5–9
Saccharum, 1–3
Schizachyrium, 3–7
Schoenoplectus, 1–5
Sesleria, 5–9
Setaria, 1–11
Sorghastrum, 3–7
Spartina, 1–3
Sporobolus, 3–5
Spodiopogon, 3–5
Stipa, smaller forms such as *S. barbata* and *S. pennata*, 3–5
Stipa, larger forms such as *S. gigantea*, 1–3
Tridens, 3–5
Typha, 1–5
Uncinia, 5–7

REFERENCES

Bornstein, Carol, Fross, David and O'Brien, Bart. *California Native Plants for the Garden.* Los Olivos, California: Cachuma Press, 2005.

Chatto Beth. *The Damp Garden* (New Edition): London: Orion, 1998.

Chatto, Beth. *The Dry Garden* (New Edition). London: Orion, 1998.

Chatto, Beth. *The Beth Chatto Handbook: A Descriptive Catalogue of Unusual Plants.* Essex, UK: Beth Chatto Gardens, 2004.

Cope, Tom and Gray, Alan. *Grasses of the British Isles.* London: Botanical Society of the British Isles, 2009.

Darke, Rick. *The American Woodland Garden.* Portland, Oregon and London: Timber Press, 2007.

Darke, Rick. *The Encyclopedia of Grasses for Livable Landscapes.* Portland, Oregon and London: Timber Press, 2007.

Dunnett, Nigel and Clayden, Andy. *Rain Gardens.* Portland, Oregon and London: Timber Press, 2007.

Dunnett, Nigel and Kingsbury, Noël. *Planting Green Roofs and Living Walls: Revised and Updated Edition.* Portland, Oregon and London: Timber Press, 2008.

Greenlee, John. *Meadows by Design: Creating a Natural Alternative to the Traditional Lawn.* Portland, Oregon and London: Timber Press, 2009.

Grounds, Roger. *Grasses: Choosing and Using these Ornamental Plants in the Garden.* London: Quadrille Publishing Ltd., 2005.

King, Michael and Oudolf, Piet. Gardening with Grasses. London: Frances Lincoln, 1998.

Lloyd, Christopher. *Meadows (New Edition).* London: Cassell Illustrated, 2004.

Mabey, Richard. *Flora Britannica: The Definitive New Guide to Britain's Wild Flowers, Plants and Trees.* London: Sinclair-Stevenson., 1996.

Oehme, Wolfgang and Van Sweden, James. *Bold Romantic Gardens.* Spacemaker Press, 1998

Oudolf, Piet and Gerritsen, Henk. *Planting the Natural Garden.* Portland, Oregon and London: Timber Press, 2003.

Oudolf, Piet and Kingsbury, Noël. *Designing with Plants.* London: Conran Octopus Ltd., 1999.

Phillips, Roger and Rix, Martyn. *Perennials: Volume 1, Early Perennials* (New Edition). London: Pan Books, 1993.

Phillips, Roger and Rix, Martyn. *Perennials: Volume 2, Late Perennials* (New Edition). London: Pan Books, 1993.

Polunin, Oleg and Wright, Robin Southey. *A Concise Guide to the Flowers of Britain and Europe.* Oxford and New York: Oxford University Press, 1988.

Robinson, William. *The Wild Garden.* Sagapress, 1895.

Snodgrass Edmund C. and Snodgrass, Lucie L. *Green Roof Plants.* Portland, Oregon and London: Timber Press, 2006.

Tallamy, Douglas W. *Bringing Nature Home.* Portland, Oregon and London: Timber Press, 2007.

Wiley, Keith. O*n the Wild Side: Experiments in New Naturalism.* Portland, Oregon and London: Timber Press, 2004.

RESOURCES

UNITED STATES

The Calflora Database is a nonprofit organization providing information about California plant biodiversity for use in education, research and conservation. www.calflora.org

The California Invasive Plant Council site contains much information about invasive plants in California's precious natural areas. www.cal-ipc.org

The California Native Grasslands Association has a lot of information on native grasslands and how to preserve and protect them. www.cnga.org

The California Native Plant Society works to protect California's native plant heritage and preserve it for future generations. www.cnps.org

The California Society for Ecological Restoration is a non-profit membership-based organization dedicated to bringing about the recovery of damaged California ecosystems. www.sercal.org

The Centre for Biological Diversity works towards protecting biodiversity, with field offices in various states. www.biologicaldiversity.org

The mission of the Lady Bird Johnson Wildflower Center is to increase the sustainable use and conservation of native wildflowers, plants and landscapes. Look for the Native Plant information network. www.wildflower.org

NatureServe Explorer is an authoritative source for information on more than 70,000 plants, animals and ecosystems of the United States and Canada—with particularly in-depth coverage of rare and endangered species. www.natureserve.org/explorer

PlantRight lists invasive plants, and suggests non-invasive plants for use in different areas of California. www.plantright.org

The Plants Database provides standardized information about the vascular plants, mosses, liverworts, hornworts and lichens of the United States and its territories. Here you will find native plants listed state by state. www.plants.usda.gov

UNITED KINGDOM

The Botanical Society of the British Isles is the leading scientific society in Britain and Ireland for the study of plant distribution and taxonomy. Click on Resources for a county-by-county list of plants native to or found in those areas. Click Countries for European organizations. www.bsbi.org.uk

Buglife is Europe's only organization devoted to the conservation of all invertebrates. Their site has lots of useful information on bugs. www.buglife.org.uk

The flora of the Channel Islands is recorded on www.flora.org.gg.

The Grasslands Trust is the only national charity working specifically to protect the UK's wildflower-rich grasslands. www.grasslands-trust.org

Kew Grassbase is a great reference for researching grasses. www.kew.org/data/grassbase/index.html

The National Biodiversity Network gathers and records information on biodiversity. Click NBN Gateway for distribution of native species. www.nbn.org.uk

The Natural History Museum's excellent Web site contains the Postcode Plants database; just type in your postcode to find plants native to your area. www.nhm.ac.uk/nature-online/life/plants-fungi/postcode-plants/intro.html

EUROPE

The European Dry Grassland Group is a network of dry grassland researchers and conservationists in Europe. www.edgg.org

INDEX OF PLANT NAMES

Page numbers in *italics* refer to photographs.